THE ART
OF WINNING
COMMITMENT

THE ART OF WINNING COMMITMENT

10 Ways Leaders Can Engage Minds, Hearts, and Spirits

Dick Richards

AMACOM

American Management Association

New York • Atlanta • Brussels • Chicago • Mexico City • San Francisco
Shanghai • Tokyo • Toronto • Washington, D.C.

Special discounts on bulk quantities of AMACOM
books are available to corporations, professional
associations, and other organizations. For details,
contact Special Sales Department, AMACOM, a
division of American Management Association,
1601 Broadway, New York, NY 10019.
Tel.: 212-903-8316. Fax: 212-903-8083.
Web site: www.amacombooks.org

This publication is designed to provide accurate and authoritative information in regard to
the subject matter covered. It is sold with the understanding that the publisher is not engaged
in rendering legal, accounting, or other professional service. If legal advice or other expert
assistance is required, the services of a competent professional person should be sought.

Library of Congress Cataloging-in-Publication Data

Richards, Dick, 1943–
    The art of winning commitment : 10 ways leaders can engage minds,
hearts, and spirits / Dick Richards.
        p.   cm.
Includes bibliographical references and index.
    ISBN 0-8144-0785-4 (hardcover)
    1. Employee motivation.   2. Employee loyalty.   3. Organizational
commitment.   4. Commitment (Psychology)   I. Title.

    HF5549.5.M63R535 2004
    658.3'14—dc22

                                                                    2003019964

Printing number

10   9   8   7   6   5   4   3   2   1

For Melanie

Contents

Acknowledgments

The core of this book—a set of leadership competencies for inspiring mind, heart, and spirit—was forged in the domain that encompasses experience, observation, reflection, and application. The book is a result of more than three decades of consulting, coaching, and training leaders and prospective leaders in over fifty organizations and in more than a dozen countries. It owes much to all of the clients and friends who generously shared their stories and their challenges, and who invited me on their expeditions to develop their leadership abilities.

The seed of the book was an electronic document nurtured in partnership with my friend and colleague Rick McKnight, and first brought to the marketplace by Tom Brown, a pioneer internet publisher. John Willig, who is my literary agent, encouraged the document to become a book and found a home for it. Adrienne Hickey, acquisitions editor for AMACOM, recognized it as a valuable contribution to the literature of leadership, and Christina McLaughlin and Erika Spelman patiently and sensitively guided it into this its present form. I am grateful to all of them.

Twenty leaders and leadership thinkers stepped forward to share their stories and insights: Odds Bodkin, Matt Catingub, Wesley Clark, Kathy Covert, Pat Croce, Jim Ellis, Vincent Francia, Dale Fushek, Dawn Gutierrez, Alice Harris, Mary Ellen Hennen, David Hollister, Marvin Israelow, Michael Jones, Wilma Mankiller, Beverly O'Neill, Zalman Schachter-Shalomi, Bill Strickland, Jim Wold, and Bonnie Wright. Whenever the writing bogged down I returned to their ideas and experiences and found inspiration. I am grateful to all of them as well.

Others gave invaluable assistance by connecting me with those who agreed to be interviewed, or by offering advice and counsel, or by reading and commenting on early drafts. For those things, great thanks go to Linne Bourget, Bob Canady, George Davis, Kathryn Hall, Nick Head, Bob Paull, Norman Schwartzkopf, Christine Whitney-Sanchez, Mike Wold, and Alan Zaklad.

And then there is Melanie Richards—my amazing and brilliant wife. I have relied on her unflagging drive to scout for information, people, and opportunities, and for finding just the right note in this writing. I have depended on her patience, understanding, creativity, and love. For all of those things, and for much more, I am deeply grateful.

THE ART
OF WINNING
COMMITMENT

Democracy, Leadership, and Commitment

O n May 22, 1782, just six years after the signing of the Declaration of Independence, U.S. Army Colonel Lewis Nicola, frustrated by the inability of the fledgling American Congress to raise funds to pay the army, wrote to President George Washington urging him to become king of the United States. Washington's refusal was adamant. He wrote back to Nicola on the same day: "If you have any regard for your country, concern for yourself or posterity, or respect for me . . . banish these thoughts from your mind, and never communicate, as from yourself, or any one else, a sentiment of the like nature."[1]

Nicola's desire for a sovereign ruler and Washington's rebuff reflect the early stages of a shift in human consciousness, and a revolution in human expectations about leadership. Nicola's urgings were in tune with previous human experience and with the inclination of human consciousness at that time. Until the early years of the twentieth century, enthroning a sovereign, a king or perhaps an emperor, was *the thing* for new nations to do. Greece enthroned a king in 1829, Belgium in 1831, Norway in 1908, and Albania in 1913. The ill-fated King Faisal was installed by the British as the ruler of Iraq in 1921. Colonel Nicola was simply deferring to an impulse that continues in some places today, more than 200 years later. The impulse to sovereignty still holds sway in many organizations, and in recent years some business leaders have behaved like the worst of sovereigns, robbing the treasury to meet their own twisted needs at the expense of their "subjects."

Democracy's Century

A 1999 report by Freedom House pointed out that there were no true electoral democracies as late at the beginning of the twentieth century. Some countries, such as the United States and Britain, did have electoral systems, but large segments of their citizenry were denied the right to vote. Things had changed by the middle of the century, when 31 percent of the world's population lived in 22 democratic nations. By the end of the century, 62.5 percent lived in 120 democracies, causing Freedom House to dub the 1900s as *Democracy's Century*. Freedom House described this dramatic shift as one of "a growing global human rights and democratic consciousness."[2]

This shift has demanded leadership that is increasingly more respectful toward those being led: from the dismissive declaration, "Let them eat cake," which is most often attributed to Marie Antoinette, to Herbert Hoover's patriarchal promise of, "A chicken in every pot," to Martin Luther King's as yet unfulfilled vision of all people singing together, "Free at last! Free at last!"

Ancient wisdom about leadership is generally immaterial to the democratic consciousness. For example, Sun-Tzu's *The Art of War*, written about 500 B.C., advises leaders to regard their soldiers as their children. He and Renaissance philosopher Nicolo Machiavelli both extolled the virtues of deceit and firm discipline. But the volume and rapidity of modern communication, the ease of access to information and to varying opinions, along with an increase in literacy and sophistication in the world population, have all conspired to render humankind less susceptible to deceit. Democracy has made us less responsive to the firm discipline of those who would behave as sovereigns. Much of what the old texts advise does not play well today.

We have become more difficult to lead. Another consequence of democratic consciousness is that acceptance of any particular authority is more optional than it once was. Political leaders can be voted in or out of office, new jobs can be found, with new bosses, and there is a different brand of religion in a synagogue, church, or mosque just around the corner. Today, we no longer rely on only two or three authoritative network news anchors to translate the world's events for us—cable television provides a plethora of authorities. The Internet has made it possible for each of us to develop our own authoritative voice by making ever more information and knowledge readily available, and by giving each of us a platform to reach the whole world with our own unique message.

The factors that have made us more difficult to lead provide, on the other hand, leadership opportunities. The ascendance of democratic consciousness is marked by liberation of the whole person—thought, feeling, and spirit. Thus, today's leaders must be capable of dealing with all facets of the whole person. This complexity is sometimes problematic because people are so very complex, yet it is also an opportunity because people who are able to *be* so much more themselves are able to *commit* so much more. Followers have grown up, and leaders must grow up as well.

Where We Have Been

In the middle of *Democracy's Century*, leadership theorists such as Warren Bennis, Kurt Lewin, Peter Drucker, Douglas McGregor, and Chris Argyris began to examine leadership in the context of the new democratic consciousness. The leadership thinkers of the middle and latter half of the twentieth century saw the relationship between a leader and his followers through eyes that were more resonant with the new reality.

Near the end of the century, however, in 1989, Bennis asked, "Where have all the leaders gone?" He answered the question with a refrain from a popular folk song: "long time passing."[3] Bennis decried the loss of such leadership greats as Churchill, Schweitzer, Einstein, Gandhi, the Kennedys, and Martin Luther King. It is as if a group of great leaders emerged in the middle of *Democracy's Century*, then great leadership disappeared, and we have been trying ever since to figure out what they did so that we might replicate it.

Bennis also reminded us that we need leaders because they take responsibility for the effectiveness and integrity of our institutions, and because they serve as both heralds and beacons for our common purposes. We do need leaders, but we need a different brand of leader from those who governed as sovereign rulers and perhaps even from those who captured our imaginations during the time of transition from sovereignty to democracy.

Admirable leadership does still show up on the world stage from time to time when someone such as Rudy Giuliani leads New York City's response to the September 11th terrorist attacks on the World Trade Center. But this kind of leadership is driven by crisis. As dramatic and profound as it may be, it is also occasional and fleeting, riveting us for only a few days or a few weeks. A devastating conflagration in the dry mountains of Arizona introduces us to a dynamic hard-hatted master of fire management. When the fire is extinguished, he is gone. An imposing general emerges triumphant from a brief war to free a tiny country— Kuwait. When victory is achieved, he no longer commands headlines. The shooting-star brilliance of leaders such as these reminds us of what has passed from the fabric our lives, but is not enough to create and sustain change, nor to meet the many ongoing challenges of our time.

Like a long lost friend, in the absence of sustained leadership we are in danger of forgetting its face. Each Martin Luther King Day, we watch grainy black-and-white film footage of Dr. King extolling his dream. The setting on the steps of the Lincoln Memorial, the rhythm of his speech, the power of his words, are still captivating—"Let freedom ring." In cable programming and in films we watch actors portraying John and Robert Kennedy agonize over the Cuban missile crisis. We observe these images in much the same way we might page through an old photograph album. If we are old enough, we watch with nostalgia and a hint of longing. If we are young enough, we dismiss the relevance of the past, or we try to imagine what it was like to be among those giants. The images show us what has passed, but in our mind's eye Gandhi looks like Ben Kingsley; not quite the real thing, only an approximation—an actor strolling the banks of the Ganges.

Where We Are

Since Bennis warned us that leadership was lacking, recovering it has acquired the aspect of a legitimate obsession. A recent Internet search for the term "leadership" turned up 10.3 million Web pages in a brisk twelve one-hundredths of a second. A search using the more narrow term "research about leadership" turned up more than 2.5 million pages: colleges and universities, institutes, consultants, foundations, training organizations, in business, communities, health care, government, education, the military, the arts, and the sciences. In short—everywhere. Another search for the term "leadership" at a popular online bookseller turned up more than 12,000 books.

With all of this attention, one might think we understand leadership much better than we once did. But some evidence does not support that assumption. A 1996 study of the use of the terms "leader" and "leadership" in a sample of both general interest and special interest American publications concluded that, "there is no specific definition of what a leader is, who the leaders are, what leadership is, or even if it is necessary to define these terms in only one way."[4]

In addition, the researchers concluded, "There also appears to be an assumption of a common understanding of what a leader is and what characteristics are needed for leadership." A more recent (but far less rigorous) scanning of newspapers and magazines gives no cause to believe these conclusions about our collective understanding of leadership have changed since 1996. For example, one newspaper uses the term "leadership" in headlines that accompany stories about people who speak out publicly about a controversial issue. Is the mere act of speaking out "leadership?" Or is something more required to earn that label? We have no consensus about what leadership means, but we think and act as if we do.

A Definition of Leadership

Leadership has become one of those phenomena we discuss while assuming we understand what it is we are discussing, and while assuming those we are talking with are speaking of the same thing. However, more often than we know, we and they have something quite different in mind. When we talk of leadership, we ought to be clear about what we mean. In this book . . .

> *leadership means inspiring others*
> *to commit their energy to a common purpose.*

This definition does not account for those leaders whose influence derives from their theories or talents in specialized fields—leaders such as Albert Einstein and Margaret Mead. This book is addressed to leaders and prospective leaders whose mission is change, and who pursue that mission by deliberately setting out to alter the paths of organizations, institutions, and lives. It contains practical wisdom to help leaders develop the competencies needed to lead people whose lives are imbued with democratic consciousness.

Who Are These Leaders?

The emphasis in this book is on how leaders can win extraordinary commitment from others. It was written primarily for leaders in business, but one feature of the book renders it also valuable for anyone with leadership responsibility or leadership aspirations. None of the twenty people interviewed for this book is a business leader in the traditional sense of the term, and none of them learned leadership skills in the traditional way that business leaders do—at a business school or a corporate university.

Those who were interviewed are all recognized leaders or people who, by virtue of a particular expertise, have something important to say about leadership. Each of them is thoughtful and articulate about leadership. Each of them has, in one way or another, achieved extraordinary results. They are an eclectic group of people. Three plow the field of education: Dawn Gutierrez, Marvin Israelow, and Jim Wold. One, Pat Croce, is a physical therapist and sports executive. Two are retired from military careers: Wesley Clark and Jim Ellis. Two are clerics: Monsignor Dale Fushek and Rabbi Zalman Schachter-Shalomi. Three—David Hollister, Vincent Francia, and Beverly O'Neill—are or have been mayors. One was chief of the Cherokee Nation—Wilma Mankiller. Three head or headed not-for-profit social service organizations: Alice Harris, Bill Strickland, and Bonnie Wright. One—Matt Catingub—conducts an orchestra. Two work in public service: Kathy Covert and Mary Ellen Hennen. Two have special expertise that is important to leadership: storyteller Odds Bodkin and pianist Michael Jones. Each of them will be introduced in more detail during the course of the book. A slightly more detailed list is included in the resources section at the back of the book. Except where otherwise noted, all quotes attributed to them are from interviews conducted by the author from January through June 2003.

The decision to focus on insights about leadership from leaders outside the realm of business arose from the belief that developing the capacity to lead in a business environment would benefit greatly from something other than more *case studies* and *best practices* of business leaders. We can learn only so much by studying what other people have done when the people we study are very much like we are, and when they inhabit environments very much like our own. Often, we can learn the most from people who are unlike us.

The people who are featured in this book, as a whole group, are less fettered by the prejudice of business, which favors intellect at the expense of emotion and spirit. Since those of us who live with a democratic consciousness are able to offer more of ourselves—higher commitment—leaders of businesses ought to capitalize more often on that bounty. They can do so by stretching themselves beyond their prejudice in favor of intellect. The people who speak in the chapters that follow know a lot about how leaders can win emotion and spirit as well as intellect.

A second feature of this book renders it especially useful now. While we already have a great deal of very wise thinking on the matter of leadership, it is fragmented and profits from being subjected to a synthesis. Leadership theory is fragmented because those of us who study it (including me) are peering through our own particular lenses. The best lenses on leadership, like any high-quality lens, provide unique pictures that are both accurate and incomplete. This book provides a synthesis of what has been seen through three different lenses; one looking at the intellectual aspect of leading, another at the emotional aspect, and the third at the spiritual aspect. Democratic consciousness allows for the possibility that people will commit mind, heart, and spirit to their leaders, so leaders who wish to win high levels of commitment must develop facility with all three.

How to Use This Book

At the heart of this book reside ten competencies for leaders to master in order to inspire mind, heart, and spirit in others—to win different levels of commitment. Chapter 1 provides an overview of the competencies and an examination of the lifeblood of leadership—commitment. Chapters 2 through 11 each treat one competency, defining it, describing it, and offering advice for leaders who wish to improve in that particular competency. Few leaders master all ten competencies; that task is truly daunting. However, when familiar with the competencies, any leader ought to be able to identify those which she needs to focus on or develop *now*. The final chapter offers additional general advice about how to go about mastering the competencies.

The book is organized sequentially, beginning with an overview of the competencies in Chapter 1, then describing each in turn, finishing with the last—centering—which is the competency that brings everything else together. Readers who prefer to see the whole picture before delving into details may want to read chapters 1, 11, and 12 first.

At the end of each of the ten chapters that describe a competency, there are four questions to contemplate or to discuss with trusted others. In general, these questions ask:

1. Who, in your life experience, was practiced at the competency?
2. To what degree are you practiced at the competency?
3. What is it about the competency that rings true for your current leadership role?
4. How important is the competency to your further development as a leader?

Where the answer to the last question is "very important," you will find specific advice in the form of "development strategies" within the chapter, and general advice about learning to lead in Chapter 12. The lists of development strategies are not intended as comprehensive inventories, but as beginning suggestions.

While the book is grounded partly in the observation that the development of leadership must keep pace with the growing democratic consciousness, it contains no insinuation that all human organizations ought to be fully democratic. However, leaders of today's organizations will be well served by acknowledging that people carry a growing democratic consciousness to the organizations that they choose, expecting leaders to behave less like sovereign rulers than they have in the past. Where business leaders behave like sovereigns they are likely to hear from employee satisfaction surveys that they are not communicating, that they seem remote, that they make decisions others either don't understand or don't support, that they don't seem to have a vision or a strategy, or that they are uncaring and exploitive.

Colonel Nicola's suggestion that Washington become king seems arcane and almost laughable today; the preponderance of humanity has relinquished the impulse to crown a sovereign. But still we struggle to know how to lead people who are free in mind, heart, and spirit. The following chapters provide a synthesis of recent investigations of how successful leaders win minds, hearts, and spirits, joined with new insights and practical suggestions for leaders everywhere.

Notes

1. Claremont Institute, "Rediscovering George Washington," Public Broadcasting System Web site, 2002, <http://www.pbs.org/georgewashington/multimedia/heston/lewis_nicola.html>.
2. Freedom House, "Democracy's Century," December, 1999, <http://www.freedomhouse.org/reports/century.html>.
3. Warren Bennis, *On Becoming a Leader* (Reading, Mass.: Addison-Wesley, 1989): 3.
4. Unabridged Communications, "Who Leads? A Report on the Usage of Lead, Leader, and Leadership in Selected Newsprint Media in 1996," a report for Callahan, Smith & Gunter, Inc. <www.members.aol/breakthruz/leadership.html>.

1

Commitment and Change

A lot of people are waiting for Martin Luther King or Mahatma
Gandhi to come back—but they are gone. We are it. It is up to us.
It is up to you.

—MARIAN WRIGHT EDELMAN

A leader sounds a call to summon others. The call is a plea for
commitment to a purpose that is defined, embodied, and sym-
bolized by who that leader is and by what he says and does. The
commitment that is summoned is often a transformational power, a force
that can create substance out of mere dreams and promises through the
dedication, involvement, and persistence of those who offer it. The commitment of others is the fulfillment of the leader's art; without the commitment of others, a leader is just a voice.

Because leaders cannot lead without the commitment of others, understanding commitment in its various forms is central to their purposes. The four forms of commitment are:

1. *Political*—commitment to something in order to gain something else
2. *Intellectual*—commitment of the mind to a good idea
3. *Emotional*—commitment that arises out of strong feelings
4. *Spiritual*—commitment to a higher purpose

These four forms of commitment combine in various ways to make up a four-tiered hierarchy from the shallowest to the most profound. *Political commitment* is at the lowest level, *intellectual* or *emotional* commitment at the next level, the combination of *intellectual* and *emotional* commitment at the next level, and *spiritual* commitment at the highest level.[1] Figure 1-1 shows the four kinds of commitment combining to form four levels, from the shallowest at the bottom to the most profound at the top. The triangle in the figure represents the amount of human energy that becomes available as people make the various kinds of commitments described in the diagram. Given the same number of followers, the least amount of energy is generated when commitment is purely at the political level, more energy becomes available when either intellectual or emotional commitment is inspired, still more when intellectual and emotional commitments are both inspired, and the greatest amount of energy when spiritual commitment is inspired.

Although millions of Web sites and thousands of books offer guidance to leaders, the vast majority of this guidance calls attention to one of the four forms of commitment, but not to all of them. In other words, some guidance explains how to call for political commitment, some how to call for intellectual commitment, some how to call for emotional commitment, and some how to call for spiritual commitment. This book provides a synthesis that will guide any leader to judge the level of commitment needed to produce change in any given situation, to know whether or not it is possible, and what the leader might do in order to gain that form of commitment from followers.

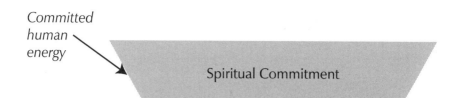

Committed human energy

Spiritual Commitment

Intellectual Commitment and Emotional Commitment

Intellectual Commitment or Emotional Commitment

Political Commitment

Figure 1-1. Four kinds of commitment at four levels, from the shallowest level at the bottom to the most profound level at the top.

Political Commitment

The shallowest form of commitment is political. It involves committing to ideas or actions when we have little or no drive to follow through because our motives have less to do with the object of our commitment, and more to do with what we might gain or avoid by offering the commitment itself. Political commitment appears in organizations when a person accepts an assignment, not out of any special feeling about its importance, nor because it seems a very good idea, but out of a desire to appear to be a "good soldier," or to get a "ticket punched" for a better assignment, or out of fear of retribution should they refuse. For example, a man who was the marketing manager for a line of food items that were, by his own admission, vastly overpriced and contained no nutritional value, was doing his job well because success was a certain route to a promotion. His commitment was not to the work itself but to career advancement. Political commitment also appears in personal life when we avoid speech or behavior merely because they are considered "politically incorrect" or when we take on the trappings of the moment because "everyone is doing it."

Political commitment is the basic fuel of most organizations. People are generally attracted to working in organizations by such promises as "good pay," "great benefits," "opportunities for advancement," and "a pleasant work environment." These are all good things to have, and the nature of working for an organization involves employees pledging to perform an honest day's work in return for them. A lot gets accomplished when those in leadership positions agree to such promises, and political commitment is usually enough to get the job done as long as everything is going smoothly.

Political commitment is usually enough when only lower-order change is needed: when people need to do more of something, or less; when only a small amount of new learning is needed; when an alternative way is sought for doing things that they already know how to do, or when adjustments are made to what already exists. Whenever a change is viewed as a necessary and normal part of the job, political commitment suffices.

A leader whose primary call is for political commitment can usually expect "an honest day's work for an honest day's pay," but not much more than that, and sometimes less. This variety of commitment is frequently halfhearted and short-lived. It lacks the oomph, verve, and sheer stubbornness needed to achieve a challenging common purpose.

Intellectual Commitment

A leader calls for intellectual commitment by asking followers to support a purpose because they are logically convinced of its value. In order to convince them, the leader constructs what cognitive psychologist Howard Gardner calls a "story." He wrote:

I view leadership as a process that occurs within the minds of individuals who live in a culture—a process that entails the capacity to create stories, to understand and evaluate these stories, and to appreciate the struggle among stories.[2]

An important component of a leader's story is a vision of the future. It is a picture that a leader draws for followers—a picture of some ideal future state. The story might also contain a rationale for why the leader's particular story is better than the story his followers now accept, or why it is better than any particular competing story.

Leaders call for intellectual commitment by both communicating and embodying their stories. The stories related by Gardner's leaders are about the leader and his followers pursuing a common quest. "Together," wrote Gardner, "they have embarked on a journey in pursuit of certain goals, and along the way and into the future, they can expect to encounter certain obstacles or resistances that must be overcome."[3]

Gardner believes that these stories are primarily about *identity*, about who the leader is and who the followers might become. One good example of such a leader is Margaret Thatcher, named by *Time Magazine* as one of the 100 most important people of the twentieth century. *Time* called her the "champion of free minds and markets."[4] Thatcher's story was of a new kind of Britain, embracing a dramatic change. She convinced the British (not all of them to be sure, but enough to elect her as Prime Minister three times) to challenge their idea of themselves, to abandon governmental interference and embrace privatization of industry and services, as well as individual initiative. She reportedly told a group of aspiring business people, "The only thing I am going to do for you is make you freer to do things for yourself. If you can't do it, I'm sorry. I'll have nothing to offer you."[5]

The British at the time were not accustomed to such talk from their leaders. Thatcher was intolerant of the socialism, bureaucracy, and powerful intransigent unions that suffused British society. Her message was clearly a different story from the one Britons had been living.

Intellectual commitment in combination with political commitment can accelerate lower-order change. If a person is politically committed to her work and a good idea presents itself, that idea will probably be pursued.

Emotional Commitment

A leader's call for emotional commitment is an appeal to gut feelings that compel people to act. Where intellectual commitment is about convincing people, winning emotional commitment is about moving them. Daniel Goleman is a psychologist whose work is about emotional intelligence, which refers to one's ability to know and manage one's emotions, motivate oneself, recognize emotions in others, and handle relationships effectively.[6] Goleman, along with Richard Boyatzis, a professor of organizational behavior, and Annie McKee, an educator and business consultant, explored the significance of Emotional Intelligence to leadership in their book *Primal Leadership*. The authors make their view of leadership very clear when they state,

> Great leadership works through the emotions . . . even if they get everything else just right, if leaders fail in this primal task of driving emotions in the right direction, nothing they do will work as well as it could or should.[7]

Goleman also points out that the evolutionary development of the human brain has furnished us with primitive and instinctive responses that may be inappropriate for a given situation in the modern world. He wrote, "For better or for worse, our appraisal of every personal encounter and our responses to it are shaped not just by our rational judgments or our personal history, but also by our distant ancestral past."[8]

Civilization has developed with a rapidity that exceeds the development of our emotional competence, says Goleman. And because emotions are impulses to act, our actions may be driven by impulses, such as anger, fear, and frustration, that are appropriate only to a time in our distant past. Emotional Intelligence is about understanding this, and also about employing our capacity to exert intelligent management of our emotions and behavior.

According to Goleman and his coauthors, leaders are *resonant* when they are able to hit just the right emotional chord with their followers so that people feel uplifted and inspired. This resonance in turn amplifies and prolongs the leader's message. Sometimes that chord begins with the leader's hope and enthusiasm. But it might also begin when the leader empathizes by tuning into and expressing whatever emotions are present. Either way, says Goleman, "Emotionally intelligent leaders build resonance by tuning into people's feelings—their own and other's—and guiding them in the right direction."[9] A leader's resonance with followers gives rise to emotional commitment.

Just as lower-order change can be accelerated by combining intellectual commitment with political commitment, so too can change be accelerated by combining emotional commitment with political commitment. If a person is politically committed and has strong feelings about a needed change, that change will probably be pursued.

Hearts and Minds Together

David Hollister has thought intently about both intellectual and emotional commitment. He was a high school teacher in the 1960s, who later served nineteen years in the Michigan house of representatives, where he was consistently recognized as a top legislator. In 1993 he ran a successful campaign for mayor of Lansing, and then was elected for a second term in a landslide win. He now leads a new state department on labor and economic growth.

Hollister contrasts those who are intellectually committed with those who are emotionally committed. Intellectually committed people grasp the significance of whatever change is being proposed in historical terms. Hollister wrote, "These people have a sophisticated understanding of the interrelationships, the nuances, and the subtleties of the situation." People who are emotionally committed have a different air: "Those with the emotional commitment are the traditional activists. They are highly motivated and are anxious 'to get involved' to try to change conditions."[10]

However, says Hollister, intellectual and emotional commitment each have limitations. The intellectually committed may not be able to move beyond thought and into action. The emotionally committed, lacking broad perspective, may not fully understand the goals to which they are committing themselves and so may engage in action that is thoughtless and off target. Figure 1-2 summarizes the value and limitations of both intellectual and emotional commitment.

So intellectual commitment by itself may breed understanding but inaction, while emotional commitment by itself may produce action that runs amok. However, gaining both intellectual and emotional commitment—winning both minds and hearts—in the service of the same purpose offers the promise of great results. Jacob Bronowski acknowledged this in *The Ascent of Man*:

> Yet every man, every civilization, has gone forward because of its engagement with what it has set itself to do. The personal commitment of a man to his skill, the intellectual and the emotional commitment working together as one, has made the Ascent of Man.[11]

For sustained change of any kind, other than that of the lowest order, the combination of intellectual and emotional commitment is the minimum commitment needed.

Commitment	Value	Limitations
INTELLECTUAL	Sophisticated understanding of the broader significance of the purpose.	Possible inaction or halfhearted action.
EMOTIONAL	Motivation to get involved—to act on the purpose.	Lacks broad perspective on the significance of the purpose. Actions may be unintentionally off-purpose.

Figure 1-2. The values and limitations of intellectual and emotional commitment.

Spiritual Commitment

There is yet a fourth form of commitment—the most profound form—spiritual commitment. As Figure 1-1 shows, this form of commitment yields the greatest amount of human energy, given the same number of followers. It was described eloquently in a keynote speech to the Mobius Leadership Forum at Harvard Business School by Deepak Chopra, who said,

> The leader . . . is the symbolic soul of a group, who acts as a catalyst for change and transformation.[12]

Chopra defines spirituality as, "A domain of awareness . . . where we experience our universal nature."[13] In this domain we recognize the commonality of all humans at the soul level. This recognition becomes the root of love, compassion, and wisdom—all necessary if a leader is calling for spiritual commitment. For Chopra the magic of leadership is found in the relationship between leader and followers; a relationship in which leaders create followers and followers create leaders.

> And so if we understand this principle that leaders and followers cocreate each other, that they form an invisible spiritual bond; that leaders exist to embody the values that followers want, and followers exist to fuel the leader's vision from inside themselves, then we begin to understand why we see the type of leaders that we see in certain situations.[14]

Such leadership is rarely seen in organizational life unless the organization itself is inherently spiritual or involves some form of helping. The term "spiritual" is used here not necessarily in the sense of "religious" but in the sense of a calling from some source larger than one's self. The call may be religious, but might also be from some other entity such as a community, a family, a set of ideals or values, or those who are in need. When we see people whose commitment attains this level, we experience them as "being on a mission." The mission is usually long-term and sometimes seems to consume the person, as if they were seized by something larger than everyday life. Spiritually committed people give of themselves selflessly and with fervor.

Unlike political commitment, the three higher forms—intellectual, emotional, and spiritual—cannot be bought or sold. They cannot be demanded or coerced. Spiritual commitment in particular evades capture by anyone other than the person who experiences it. It comes from a deeper source than most people bring to their day-to-day work, and from a place within that many people in leadership positions do not touch.

The kind of commitment leaders will attract depends on the depth at which they can tell their stories. If they are competent at articulating an idea in a compelling way, then they will draw people with intellectual commitment. If they are competent at articulating their idea in a way that also comes from the heart, then they will draw the kind of people who have heart for what they are trying to do; those who can offer emotional commitment. If they are competent at articulating an idea that comes from that deeper place within each of us—from the spirit—then they will draw spiritually oriented people who can offer the highest level of commitment. The kind and degree of commitment a leader draws depends upon her competence.

Materials of the Leader's Art

Those who expect to lead masterfully must be as versatile as was Michelangelo; they must be masters of three distinct art forms. Michelangelo fashioned the *Pieta* and the statue of *David* from blocks of raw marble, painted the vaulted ceiling of the Sistine Chapel in the Vatican, and was a primary contributor to the construction of St Peter's Basilica. He was a sculptor, a painter, and an architect: three distinct art forms. Inspiring intellectual, emotional, and spiritual commitments are each forms of art in the truest sense.

Artists work with their materials and their competencies to provoke a response from others. For example, Michelangelo employed his various materials and diverse competencies primarily to inspire awe and reverence. Leaders, although they work with far less tangible materials than Michelangelo's marble, pigment, and building matter, nonetheless also employ their various materials and diverse competencies to provoke a response—commitment.

The material used in the art of winning intellectual commitment is a *story*. The story is much more than merely a vision of what might be, or a tale about a quest for change, but is also a challenge to the very identities of followers. It is a summons to become more than they are, more than they can become by their own solitary efforts. This art calls for four competencies—*insight, vision, storytelling,* and *mobilizing*—in order to *convince* people of the story's worthiness.

The material used in the art of winning emotional commitment is *feeling*. This art calls for competencies that are far more subtle and therefore more difficult to master—*self-awareness, emotional engagement,* and *fostering hope*. Inspiring emotional commitment entails *moving* people to go the extra mile to create concrete reality out of abstract purpose.

The material used to win spiritual commitment is *soul*. Inspiring spiritual commitment is the least concrete of the three arts. The effects of storytelling and feeling can often be seen directly, while the effects of soul as it works in the relationship between a leader and followers can only be sensed in the most intangible ways; some measure of faith is required. Competencies for inspiring spiritual commitment are *rendering significance, enacting beliefs,* and *centering*. These are less solid, more numinous talents. Leaders inspire soul in order to *engage* people more fully and deeply.

A story, feeling, and soul are a leader's forms of marble, pigment, and building matter. They are the stuff out of which a leader creates art—convincing, moving, and engaging people—inspiring different forms and levels of commitment. The ten leadership competencies, along with the basic material of each and the desired response, are shown in Figure 1-3.

	Winning Intellectual Commitment	Winning Emotional Commitment	Winning Spiritual Commitment
Desired Response	**Convincing People** Ensuring that they understand the purpose they are asked to support and its underlying rationale	**Moving People** Increasing their motivation to act on the purpose they are asked to support	**Engaging People** Captivating them with a sense of higher purpose or calling
Material	**Story**	**Feeling**	**Soul**
Competencies	**Insight** Perceiving what *is* in a new way **Vision** Creating an ideal image of identity and the future **Storytelling** Presenting and embodying the vision in an unforgettable way **Mobilizing** Transforming energy into committed action	**Self-Awareness** Alertness to one's internal experiences and reactions **Emotional Engagement** Creating a flow of productive feeling **Fostering Hope** Encouraging the sense that something desirable is possible or is likely to happen	**Rendering Significance** Drawing connections to a higher meaning and purpose **Enacting Beliefs** Translating spiritual beliefs and practices into leadership activities **Centering** The discipline of bringing in rather than leaving out

Figure 1-3. Leadership competencies for inspiring intellectual, emotional, and spiritual commitment.

Ten Competencies

The ten leadership competencies form the heart of this book; each is described in a separate chapter, beginning with Chapter 2. Here are brief descriptions of each competency.

Winning Intellectual Commitment

Insight—seeing what is, in a new way. Insight is a perception about a complex set of circumstances that is deeper and clearer than what ever perception prevails at the time. It often comes suddenly. For leaders, insight is most often about the needs or aspirations of a group of people.

Vision—an ideal image of identity and the future. A vision proclaims a leader's commitment to work toward an ideal. It serves followers as a touchstone, and as a picture of where they are all going together. It also challenges them to consider who they are and who they wish to become. A vision is a leader's answer to the question, "What could be?"

Storytelling—presenting the story in an unforgettable way. A leader's story contains his vision, the rationale for the vision, and ideas about what to do in order to achieve it. The presentation of the entire story must be compelling and inspiring. The leader is part of the story and must "walk the talk" and "be the story." There is a consistency about leaders—who they are, what they do, and what they say. The story and the person support one another.

Mobilizing—transforming energy into committed action. A well-told story creates human energy. Leaders have three roles to play in transforming that energy into action: enrolling people, educating them, and helping them narrow the broad challenges described in the story into actions that they can and will perform. These three roles are enacted during an extended dialogue between the leader and followers that includes everything that happens between them.

Winning Emotional Commitment

Self-Awareness—attentiveness to one's self. Emotions, motivations, hot buttons, strengths and weaknesses, style, values, the penchants that derive from the family of origin, and from life experience—all influence any attempt at leadership. Since the very *self* of the leader is his most potent (and perhaps only) instrument, it is wise to know that self well.

Emotional Engagement—the ability to create a flow of productive feeling between the leader and her followers, and among the followers themselves. Emotional engagement depends heavily upon a leader's skill at empathy—sensing and prizing the feelings of others. A person knows a leader is empathetic when he feels heard and affirmed—not necessarily agreed with, but understood and accepted.

Fostering Hope—creating the feeling that something desirable is possible or likely to happen. A leader's ability to foster hope depends upon his optimism; the tendency to believe that right will prevail, that good will triumph over evil, that hope is a fitting response to difficult challenges. The ability to instill hope through optimism is an essential leadership task.

Winning Spiritual Commitment

Rendering Significance—drawing the connections from the leader's insight, vision, and story to a higher meaning and purpose. By rendering significance to their insights, visions, and stories leaders help people come to full human maturity through the diverse forms of their individual lives.

Enacting Beliefs—translating beliefs and principles into leadership activities, not as a religious statement, but as an endeavor of good leadership that wins high commitment.

Centering—the discipline of bringing in rather than leaving out. In a leader's contacts with followers, mind, emotion, and spirit are invited in when they show up. Centering is the competency through which a leader brings all of the other competencies together as a seamless whole.

Levels of Change

Along with understanding the nature of commitment, and with mastering the competencies for winning intellectual, emotional, and spiritual commitment, a leader needs to ask and answer the question: What level of commitment is needed to effect the change that I am seeking? The answer is dependent upon the level of change involved. The lowest level of change demands little more than new behavior—doing something better for example, or doing it in a new way, or finding a fix for a problem in an existing system without changing the nature of the system itself. At this level of change, things chug along in first gear. The lowest level of change can usually be accomplished with political commitment, and can be accelerated by either intellectual or emotional commitment.

Higher levels of change involve shifting gears upward. They require learning and looking at things in new ways. The nature of the system itself must change: A society relinquishes dependence on institutions in favor of individual initiative, democracy replaces dictatorship, a life insurance company becomes a full-service financial company, aging people transform themselves into a force for change, an arrogant industry embraces customer service. In changes such as these, a whole new story begins. Rather than applying remedies, something new will be generated. Such change transforms systems: A new lifestyle is adopted, a conversion occurs, the identity of those involved changes, not just their behavior, and the understanding of how the system works is revolutionized. Sometimes, something more than learning is required—perhaps rethinking the very ground of learning, asking how we learn, or adopting a whole new way of learning.

Higher levels of change necessitate challenging old beliefs and adopting new ones, or they offer a test of identity, or they call for the trials and sacrifice that accompany passion. This kind of change requires at least the amalgamation of intellectual and emotional commitment, and perhaps commitment that can flow only from the spirit.[15]

Self and Situation

There is debate among leaders and leadership thinkers about whether it is possible to construct a list of ideal leadership traits, skills, or competencies, or whether the ability of any one person to lead depends upon the situation in which leadership is needed. The answer to this dilemma ought to reside in science; yet so far science has not developed instruments sensitive enough to catalogue or measure the totality of human qualities and behaviors needed for leadership or accurately described the complexity of any given human situation. Leadership is profoundly philosophical and psychological, and therefore eludes scientific analysis.

The position here is that leadership is an art that can be informed by science. Painters understand the chemistry of paint, photographers, the physics of light, and dancers, the potential and limits of human anatomy—they each know what science can tell them about their art. However, they also keenly observe what competencies, skills, and attitudes their situation requires, what others are doing, what works and what does not. And they spend countless hours practicing.

Think of the competencies that are described here as a suggested color palette for plying the leader's art. Depending on the purpose of the art and on its subject, each competency might be more or less important from situation to situation. But the three questions the painter asks are the same as those a leader must ask.

1. *What does this scene require?* A seascape needs a painter who is proficient at capturing movement; a company that must rise out of pain and cynicism will first need a leader who can engage emotionally. A desert scene needs a painter who is proficient at depicting openness; a directionless organization will first need a leader with insight, a compelling vision, and a good story. As the scene changes, the painter needs a different proficiency, the leader, a different competency.

2. *Have I developed the competency to do what the scene requires?* Honest self-assessment is needed here!

3. *If not, how can I develop the competency I need?* Each of the following chapters contains specific suggestions for developing the competency the chapter describes. The final chapter gives more general suggestions about developing, honing, and refining leadership.

While reading the following chapters, be alert to those competencies that will enable you to lead in a way that makes the best use of who you are. Note those competencies that will make your leadership more personally fulfilling and that will best suit the organization you lead.

Summary

The commitment that leaders seek and that forms the lifeblood of their leadership, arrives in four forms—political, intellectual, emotional, and spiritual. These forms of commitment combine in various ways to create different levels of energy that can become available to a leader's purposes, the lowest level being political commitment, the highest level being spiritual commitment. Leaders appeal to higher levels of commitment by practicing the arts involved in inspiring intellectual, emotional, and spiritual commitment, each of which depends upon a different set of competencies.

Notes

1. I came across the four-forms model of commitment many years ago and its origins are lost, at least to me. Variations of the model are used by many authors.
2. Howard Gardner, *Leading Minds: An Anatomy of Leadership* (N.Y.: BasicBooks, 1995): 22.
3. Ibid, 14.
4. Paul Johnson, "The Most Important People of the 20th Century: Margaret Thatcher," *Time Magazine*, at <http://time.com/time/time100/leaders/profile/thatcher.html> (August, 2003).
5. Margaret Thatcher is quoted in Gardner, *Leading Minds*, 236.
6. Daniel Goleman, *Emotional Intelligence* (N.Y.: Bantam Books, 1995): 43.
7. Daniel Goleman, et al., *Primal Leadership* (Boston: Harvard Business School Press, 2002): 3.
8. Goleman, *Emotional Intelligence*, 5.
9. Goleman, et al., *Primal Leadership*, 26.
10. David Hollister, *On Organizing* <www.educ.msu.edu/epfp/dh/main.htm>.
11. Jacob Bronowski, *The Ascent of Man* (Boston: Little Brown, 1973): 438.
12. Deepak Chopra in a speech to the Mobius Leadership Forum annual conference at the Harvard Business School, April 11–12, 2002. <http://www.mobiusforum.org/deepak.htm> (November, 2002).
13. Ibid.
14. Ibid.
15. The discussion of levels of change has its foundations in the various writing of Gregory Bateson about *orders of change* and of Robert Dilts about *logical levels*.

PART 1

WINNING INTELLECTUAL COMMITMENT

A LEADER'S ABILITY TO WIN INTELLECTUAL COMMITMENT DE-pends on her facility at convincing others to support a purpose because that purpose is intellectually appealing—it is a good idea. Intellectually committed people act upon the purpose because they are logically convinced of its value. The use of the term intellectual to describe this form of commitment does not mean solely rational analysis, but rather the entire spectrum of intellectual activity: creativity, imagination, reflection, and so forth. It includes both the divergent forms of thinking, such as brainstorming and other activities intended to fire our minds, and the convergent forms such as synthesis.

There are four leadership competencies involved in winning intellectual commitment: *insight, vision, storytelling,* and *mobilizing* the energy of others. The first two competencies—insight and vision—are preconditions that enable a leader to engage intellectually with followers. The vehicle for engagement is the leader's "story." The telling of the story then provides intellectual energy that can be mobilized and converted into action. This process is shown in Figure Part 1-1.

Figure Part 1-1. The process of winning intellectual commitment.

Intellectual commitment is the kind of commitment that is most often sought by leaders, particularly in organizations where intellect is highly prized. Although it is essential for leaders who want to win high levels of commitment to seek intellectual commitment, this kind of commitment alone is not enough to produce significant and sustainable change.

2

Insight

The intuitive mind is a sacred gift and the rational mind is a faithful servant. We have created a society that honors the servant and has forgotten the gift.

—ALBERT EINSTEIN

The genius of leadership lies in the capacity to look beyond the immediate circumstances and imagine the possibilities. Leaders who win high commitment are creative people, open to new experiences and new ways of thinking; they welcome possibility and potential, are able to tolerate the ambiguity of the creative process, and make connections where none seem to exist. This capacity to see beyond what is and to glimpse possibilities acts like radar, scanning the horizon of the leader's world and exploring the depths of a leader's experience. This combination of scanning the horizon and exploring the depths draws forth the insights that are the seeds of winning commitment from others. The first kind of scanning—toward the horizon of their world—involves an unquenchable urge to look into the future, to imagine what is possible. Listen closely to any leader, especially when she is speaking personally and informally, and you will consistently hear expressions of hopes and dreams, goals for future projects, the next steps in an ongoing venture, a description of an ideal world or society, or perhaps concerns and plans for her own future. You may hear the word "beyond" often. This capacity, to see beyond the immediate horizon, is usually called *vision* and is viewed by many as the central characteristic of leadership. Vision is the ability to create a compelling picture of a desirable future. However, there is an important and vastly overlooked precondition for vision. It is *insight.*

Insight arrives because of the second way in which the genius of leadership stretches a leader's thinking. Before any of us can see beyond what is, we must faithfully see what *is,* and then see it in a new way. Leaders peer beneath the surface of things, catching sight of subterranean levels of meaning within ordinary events and circumstances, or seeing the familiar in new and surprising ways. Again, listen carefully to the personal and informal talk of any leader and you will also hear curious and heartfelt examination of the deeper significance of the moment's important happenings. Insight is not mere observation, but a perception that penetrates beneath the accepted surface, providing a clear and deep understanding of a complex set of circumstances or seemingly disconnected information. It often comes suddenly. A leader's insight is that kind of clear, and deep, and sometimes sudden perception that is specifically about the needs or aspirations of a group of people. A vision is the culmination of a process that begins with insight.

An insight is not merely a good idea, nor is it a conclusion based on rational analysis. An insight is visceral—in the gut. And it is inspiring—in the spirit. Insights may arrive after intellectual analysis, but they are beyond intellectual analysis. A good idea that arises solely from intellectual analysis may win intellectual commitment, but it takes the compelling force of an insight to win emotional and spiritual commitment.

Bill Strickland is both a leader and an artist who sees clearly the value of insight to the leader's art. Strickland grew up in Pittsburgh's North Side. He was much like other teenagers in the predominately African-American neighborhood. He described himself as "walking around in a sixteen-year-old's haze" until he was enthralled by the sight of a skilled potter working at his wheel and decided that he too would learn the potter's art. Today, over forty years later, he is still in North Side as president and CEO of Manchester Craftsmen's Guild and the Bidwell Training Center, and he continues working as a potter. Strickland founded the guild in 1968 to help combat the economic and social ills of the community, and was later asked to take the reins of the training center. Today these two institutions offer model education programs in a 62,000 square foot vocational training and arts center, offering programs in such varied disciplines as chemistry, culinary arts, horticulture, and information sciences. Strickland's wisdom about the relationship between social change, entrepreneurship, and the arts is much sought after, and he served on the board of the National Endowment for the Arts.[1]

Strickland defined insight as, "The ability to perceive relationships that are not obvious or apparent." He offered the image of a painter as an example: "An artist sits down and looks at a canvas and sees this fabulous painting. Twenty other people say 'I don't see anything.' The painter says, 'It is right here.'" When an insight visits a person, said Strickland, "They see things that other people don't see. They are right there in front of your face, but are not being observed."

A Sudden Insight

Some insights seem to arrive suddenly and intact like a blinding flash of lightning. Others seem to grow and mature more slowly like the dawning of day. The experience of Monsignor Dale Fushek provides an illustration of how an insight might arrive suddenly and of the impact such an insight can have on a leader. Fushek is the founder and former President and CEO of Life Teen, Inc., an organization that provides opportunities for teens to develop their Catholic faith. From a small initial gathering in a single church hall, Life Teen has developed into an international organization with chapters in thirteen countries, and was a primary catalyst in the gathering of half a million teenagers for the World Youth Day celebration with Pope John Paul II in Toronto in 2002.

Monsignor Fushek gained the insight that blossomed to become Life Teen while he was in seminary. He received a dinner invitation from the family of a teenager who had decided to leave the Catholic Church. After dessert everybody else at the table vacated the dining room leaving the not-yet-Father Fushek with the teenager.

What's new?" Fushek asked.

"You know what's new," the young man replied, "That's why you are here."

"I hear you are not Catholic anymore. Why? Do you have trouble believing in the Pope?"

"No," the boy replied.

"Do you have trouble believing the moral teachings of the church?"

"Not at all. I am following them."

"Do you believe in the Eucharist—that it is really the body of Christ in communion?"

"You have to. It is right there in the Bible."

"Does your new church believe that?"

"I don't know. They never mentioned it."

A bewildered and frustrated Fushek then asked, "If you believe in the Pope, and you believe in the moral teachings of the church, and you believe in the Eucharist, what are you doing?"

The young man looked Fushek in the eye and said, "For the sixteen years of my life, never once did I miss mass on Sunday. And never once when I was there did I ever feel loved. I don't know what these new people believe, but I do know that they love me."

The now Monsignor Fushek says, "This was a life-changing experience for me. I went home that night and I said: If I become a priest I will do everything I can to make sure that no kid walks away because they don't feel loved."

Dale Fushek did not—could not—envision the scope of Life Teen at that dinner table, or at any time soon afterward. It can be reasonably argued that he has never envisioned it, even in the years since that fateful dinner. He began with an insight, not a vision, and started a movement that just kept growing. "When I did become a priest," he says, "I asked: How do you create an environment where kids feel loved?" He held a meeting in a church hall, then subsequent meetings attracted more teens, and soon other parishes were calling to ask, "How did you do that?" At the end of 2002, Life Teen had over 800 programs worldwide, reaching over 100,000 teens weekly.

Less Sudden Insight

Not every leader's insight is as sudden as Dale Fushek's. Some arise out of study and reflection. In 1875, when Mark Twain was busy writing *Tom Sawyer* and the first useful electric light was just an idea in Thomas Edison's mind, John Fairfield Dryden and a few partners began what would come to be known as Prudential Insurance Company (now Prudential Financial) in a basement in downtown Newark, New Jersey. It was the first company in the United States to make insurance available to working-class people.

Dryden's insight about the need for affordable insurance to mitigate the financial problems of the poor came as the result of his studies of the Prudential Assurance Company of London while he was a student at Yale. Dryden's first product was low-cost burial insurance for factory workers. One biographer speculates that Dryden's insight was influenced by his own ill health, which caused him to abandon his studies.[2] Whether his own physical difficulties were a source of his insight or not, Dryden did, like Fushek, view his enterprise in the clear and deep way that characterizes insight. He once said, "Those providing life insurance services should be Missionaries of Love."[3]

Insight from Within

Not all insights spring from experience of the outer world, as did Fushek's and Dryden's; some stem from deep self-reflection. Rabbi Zalman Schachter-Shalomi is a preeminent rabbi and teacher. He is professor emeritus at Temple University, and is well known for his work to ecumenize Western religion. Nearing the age of sixty, Reb Zalman felt "anxious and out of sorts" whenever he was alone, realizing that he was growing old. He had many unanswered questions about what to do with his later years. He went on a forty-day retreat in a rustic cabin in the Southwest to pray, meditate, write, and study. He also took many long walks. During his retreat Rabbi Zalman began "harvesting his life"— enjoying his past contributions and asking what legacy he wanted to leave. He asked himself, "If I had to die now, what would I most regret not having done? What remains incomplete in my life?"[4] He recognized these questions as those that might be, and perhaps ought to be, asked and answered by anyone his age who wished to pursue a new vision of their later years. One result of Reb Zalman's insight is the Spiritual Eldering Institute that "envisions a society in which elders make a difference as active contributors in their families and communities, and in the healing of our planet."[5]

Intuition

Insights such as those of Fushek and Schachter-Shalomi are the product of intuition—a nonrational (but not irrational) way of knowing. Because intuition is nonrational it is difficult to describe in the rational language of formal definitions; one must intuit any understanding of intuition. *Webster's Dictionary* defines intuition as *the immediate knowing or learning of something without the conscious use of reasoning*. This definition is somewhat unsatisfying because it tells us only what intuition is *without*, not what intuition is *with*.

Intuition can be thought of as a perception from within that integrates sensory data, thoughts, feelings, and unconscious information into a single object of awareness. It is the source of hunches, inspiration, creativity, gut-feelings, and surprising possibilities, and is sometimes described as the ability to see around corners. It also often comes with a compelling impulse that something is obviously the right thing to do, and so insight might give new direction to a life, and then, through a leader's efforts, to an institution, or to a society.

Some people trust intuition more than others do, and because they trust it, it develops more highly in them. Robert Sternberg, Professor of Psychology and Education at Yale University and a foremost expert on intelligence, wrote, "Successfully intelligent people recognize the limits of their rationality and are also aware of the traps into which they can fall in their thinking."[6] Such people utilize both intuition and reason when making decisions and forming solutions to problems. Joseph Chilton Pearce, a renowned expert on intelligence, creativity, and learning, says that human intuition begins to fade at about age seven if it is not purposefully developed. He wrote, "Without this intuition, we develop an intellect compulsively trying to compensate by engineering our environment and each other."[7] We thus behave as if we were living in a world we cannot trust rather than one in which our intuitive powers would naturally keep our environment fine-tuned to support our own well-being.

Pearce believes that the predominance of rationality over intuition has a steep price: We have become alienated from our ability to thrive in a system—our universe—that is infinitely open and creative. In other words, human development is not keeping pace with our awareness of the complexity of our world. Using the term *reptilian* to describe primitive brain function, Pearce says, "In this alienated state we develop intellect as an ally with the physical sensory system and its primitive defense postures, producing brilliant thought in reptilian personalities. And the more brilliant the human reptile, the more precarious our situation."[8] In such an alienated posture, intuition can be seen as highly suspect, rather than as a natural form of intelligence designed to help us respond to the world according to our own well-being.

But intuition is a primary tool of leadership, and leaders, like other artists, must not be afraid of their tools. Leaders who operate in incredibly complex environments cannot engineer success, and therefore cannot rely solely on intellect. They must trust the world in which they operate, and they must trust their intuition. In organizations that worship intellect and that require change, the more successful leaders will be those who can rise beyond intellect and employ a fusion of rationality and intuition.

Bill Strickland sees that leaders, and especially entrepreneurs, routinely rely on their intuition. "The act of taking a piece of clay that has no shape and forming it into a vessel is a pretty dramatic process," he said. "A lot of it relies on a kind of intuitive understanding of the material and a visual understanding of what is possible. I think leadership, when it is done right, is a combination of that because you are really looking at a potential problem and seeing an opportunity. Often times in ways that other people can't identify."

Strickland uses Howard Schultz, the guiding force of the Starbucks coffee empire, as an example of a person with intuitive understanding. Strickland said, "Howard Schultz comes along 100 years after Maxwell House coffee and says, 'I can create high-end venues where people will pay three times the price for the coffee and line up to do it.' How he saw that and nobody else saw that since Maxwell House is pretty amazing."

For leaders, the "intuitive understanding of the material" that Strickland refers to means appreciating the powerful yet inscrutable natures of their own artistic media—story, feeling, and soul. They are the leader's clay, the raw stuff out of which commitment is formed.

From Insight to Vision

Deepak Chopra offers a prescription for developing the kind of insight that produces a powerful vision. He said:

> If I was a leader I would look and listen using the instruments of the flesh. I would be an unbiased observer. I would feel, I would

think and analyze with my mind, and I would be with my soul. And only then I would create a vision.[9]

None of the leaders discussed in this chapter—not Monsignor Fushek, John Dryden, Bill Strickland, nor Rabbi Schachter-Shalomi—began their leadership efforts by creating a vision. They began by doing what Chopra advises as precursors to creating a vision; listening, observing, feeling, thinking, and analyzing, being with the soul. It is these activities, the insights they produce, and the compulsion to act on those insights, that form the nucleus of leadership. One need not have a well-articulated vision in order to lead.

Those who would lead too often sabotage themselves by retreating into intellect at the expense of intuition and insight. They retreat into what Joseph Chilton Pearce calls, "An intellect compulsively trying to compensate by engineering our environment and each other." They create vision without insight. The visions they produce are typically formulaic and uninspiring. As the next chapter explains, a vision that does not begin with, and is not based on, a compelling insight, no matter how well-articulated the vision is, will not likely attract high levels of commitment from others. Given a choice between the two, a compelling insight beats a well-articulated vision, hands down. A compelling insight permits us to inspire the future as it comes into view.

Development Strategies for Insight

Insight occurs when the data of the conscious mind meets the content of the unconscious. It is a phenomenon of the human creative urge. Although it cannot be manufactured, and its arrival is unpredictable, there are five activities any leader or prospective leader can engage in to stimulate insight: asking a vital question, gathering information, pondering, reflecting, and trusting intuition.

Asking a Vital Question

Dale Fushek is in seminary, and is asking himself, "What kind of priest will I be?" John Dryden asks himself something like, "How shall I earn a living and do good work at the same time?" Zalman Schachter-Shalomi asks himself, "What remains incomplete in my life?" The process that allows insight to emerge begins by filling the mind with information about a question. Such a question must be of the kind that occupies the mind and remains there, perhaps taking on the aspect of compulsion or worry. The question may make us—in Reb Zalman's words—"anxious and out of sorts."

Gathering and Pondering

It is not enough to merely gather information in order to stimulate insight. The information ought to be, metaphorically speaking, chewed and digested. It ought to be thought about—manipulated by the mind. It is said that the unconscious has no direct contact with reality, so perhaps this chewing and digesting of information allows it to seep into the place within us where our deeper selves have access, and can produce surprising and seemingly magical results. As we consciously mull the question, and the information that it attracts, the unconscious is also doing its own hidden work.

One of the more well-known stories about the effect of this mental activity involves physicist Werner Heisenberg. In 1926, Heisenberg and his fellow physicist Niels Bohr spent many long nights in Copenhagen arguing and puzzling over newly born theories of quantum mechanics. In February of 1927, Bohr left Copenhagen and Heisenberg was left behind to think alone about the exciting but disturbing questions they had been discussing.

In his writing about this period of solitude, Heisenberg described the obstacles before him as insurmountable. He wondered if he and Bohr had been asking the wrong questions. He tried to make connections between seemingly mutually exclusive facts. He recalled something that Einstein had told him, "It is the theory which decides what we can observe." Heisenberg was convinced that the key to the puzzle he had been trying to put together lay in Einstein's words. Clearly, Heisenberg was chewing and digesting. Struggling with his thoughts, he decided on a nocturnal walk in a nearby park.[10]

It was on this walk that Heisenberg formulated what is now called the uncertainty principle of quantum mechanics. It was a breakthrough that changed the world of physics. His great insight did not happen all by itself. It happened only after a long and intense period of gathering and pondering information.

Reflecting

Heisenberg's walk in the park might stand as a symbol for the reflection needed in order to allow insight to emerge. Reflection, as I am using the term here, does not mean more thinking about whatever the object of all the prior gathering and pondering might be. It means, rather, a cessation of gathering and pondering; taking a walk in the park on a dark cold winter night in Copenhagen.

Bonnie Wright now understands the need for reflecting after six months of retirement from her distinguished thirty-two-year career in a variety of leadership roles in the Red Cross, including coordinating the Red Cross response to the Loma Prieta earthquake which devastated the San Francisco and Monterey Bay areas in 1989. When asked what she wished she had done differently during her career, she said, "I would have spent some amount of time every day in reflection, getting my God-given to-do list." The quieter voice that comes from within usually emerges only during such periods of reflection; periods in which we move the switch that keeps the mind racing into the off position. Of course, there is no guarantee that insight will come. But when that voice does emerge, it seems to come from nowhere that we have recently inhabited.

Leaders must avoid considering periods of reflection as time away from their jobs. Leadership is about the big picture that does not yet exist. Since it does not yet exist it can only be reflected upon. Reflection is not time away from a leader's job; it *is* the leader's job. Bill Strickland said,

"You have to reflect on why you are doing what you are doing. Ask those kinds of questions and hopefully answer them. Or you are lost."

Unearthing a Passion

It is within the depths of what we care about most deeply that compelling insight, the very seed of leadership, is found. A compelling insight, one that stirs passion, in the hands of someone who can win commitment at all levels—intellectual, emotional, and spiritual—is a powerful force.

You already know what it is you care most deeply about. It may be buried, however, beneath those things that you must pay attention to, those things that others have told you to care about, and those things you pretend to care about for acceptance or approval or perhaps even survival. So—you already know, but you may not know that you know.

You can bring this knowledge to the surface by watching for the thing that you are most drawn to. Michael Jones is a pianist who has also been an organizational consultant and teacher for almost thirty years. He works to draw from his experience as a creator of music to discover how that experience translates into leadership. Jones put it this way: "There is something that each of us is very uniquely attracted to. Sometimes those attractions are not things that we fully understand, and they are often hard to explain." Jones suggests a way to spot what that something is. "When you can be engaged in something and three hours pass by and you think it is only fifteen minutes," he said. "That is the quality of attention that is a signal that you are probably really onto your own path." This is the thing that you think about or do, not because you must, but because you want to, or because you simply cannot help yourself— you are compelled. This is your bliss. Jones said, "We bring our heart to that." The compelling insight that can drive your leadership lies within it.

Trusting Intuition

Trusting intuition is more challenging for some people than for others. In particular, those raised in Western societies often have difficulty trusting intuition because it is not as highly prized as are rationality and analysis, and less attention is paid to developing it. We tend to mistrust that which is immeasurable. Jim Wold became superintendent of the New Richmond School District in Wisconsin in the mid-1990s. He is now executive director of the School of Education at Capella University. He has invested his work life in the field of education, and so wrestles constantly with questions about measurement. Wold said, "If you make the assumption that everything is measurable, then you are limiting all of these things that are not measurable. You are probably limiting love and emotions and passion. Because you can not measure it, does not mean it is not happening." The list of immeasurable marvels referred to by Wold also includes intuition.

Anyone can develop their intuition, and learn to trust it, by paying close attention to their responses, by relaxation, by attending to their own emotional and spiritual worlds, and by acknowledging, or at least allowing for the possibility, that there are forces at work in humankind beyond intellectual understanding. When all of this is done or is in progress, it becomes possible for a miraculous thing to occur—an insight.

Insight happens in one of two ways. We may find a piece of information that causes all of the data we have been consciously gathering to crystallize, to form a new perception. Dale Fushek's new perception was, "If I become a priest I will do everything I can to make sure that no kid walks away because they don't feel loved." John Dryden's was, "Those providing life insurance services should be Missionaries of Love." And Bill Strickland says of the students at his training center, echoing his own experience as a teenager in a socially and economically deprived neighborhood, "There is nothing wrong with the kids that come here except they don't have an opportunity to show that they are world-class citizens. Treat them that way and they will."

We may also withdraw to a place where the small voice of the unconscious can emerge from beneath the clutter of the mind. For example, Reb Zalman says that his "vision of elderhood" emerged from his retreat.[11]

Summary

Insight is the first of the four competencies through which leaders win intellectual commitment A truly compelling insight from a leader who has also mastered the competencies to bring it forth, can win emotional and spiritual commitment as well. Insight is a product of intuition, the nonrational way of knowing at the source of creativity. The arrival of an insight is unpredictable, but leaders and others can encourage insight by asking vital questions, gathering and pondering information and thoughts about the question, reflecting on what they know, and trusting their intuition to recognize when a valuable insight appears. Insight is the ground upon which the noblest and most compelling visions are constructed.

• • •

Questions About Yourself to Contemplate or Discuss with Others

Who, in your life experience, was practiced at gaining insight?

To what degree are you practiced at gaining insight?

What is it about gaining insight that rings true for your current leadership role?

How important is gaining insight to your further development as a leader?

Notes

1. Biographical information about Bill Strickland can be found at <www.bidwell-training.org> and <www.manchesterguild.org>.
2. C.R.E. Jr., "Biography of John Fairfield Dryden," in *Dictionary of American Biography* (N.Y. Scribner's, 1958): 463.
3. Bradesco Seguras, <http://www.prudentialbradesco.com.br> (January, 2002).
4. Zalman Schachter-Shalomi and Ronald S. Miller, *From Age-ing to Sage-ing: A Profound New Vision of Growing Older* (N.Y.: Warner Books, 1995): 1–3.
5. Spiritual Eldering Institute, January, 2003, <http://www.spiritualeldering.org>.

6. Robert J. Sternberg, *Successful Intelligence: How Practical and Creative Intelligence Determine Success in Life* (N.Y.: Simon & Schuster, 1996): 187.

7. Joseph Chilton Pearce, *Evolution's End: Claiming the Potential of Our Intelligence* (San Francisco: HarperSanFrancisco, 1992): 151.

8. Ibid.

9. Deepak Chopra in a speech to the Mobius Leadership Forum annual conference at the Harvard Business School, April 11–12, 2002. <http://www.mobiusforum.org/deepak.htm> (June, 2002).

10. Werner Heisenberg, *Physics and Beyond: Encounters and Conversations* (N.Y.: Harper Torchbooks, 1971): 77–78.

11. Schachter-Shalomi and Miller, *From Age-ing to Sage-ing*, 3.

3

Vision

Your vision will become clear only when you can look into your
own heart.

— CARL JUNG

he value of a compelling insight to anyone other than the person who receives it is only apparent when that person begins to
act and attracts the commitment of others. Then leadership can
begin, and a vision can serve as the magnet that attracts commitment.
Bill Strickland said about creating a vision, "The only reason I would
even bother to do it is to get the support that I need to act on the insight.
It isn't good enough to sit and have it. I am in this world and we have to
do something with these insights that applies to people living out their
lives. I have to get it down to a level where they can get hold of it even
though they do not have the benefit of the insight."

A vision is a mental picture of a desirable future. It may be stated as abstractly as Martin Luther King's "dream" or as concretely as the construction of a new corporate headquarters. It may describe a definitive outcome or product, or it may depict an ideal ongoing process. Its seeds lie within the vital question a leader asks and the compelling insight the question produces. A vision begins to answer the many additional questions and issues raised by a provocative insight.

The value of a well-articulated vision was not always as obvious as it is today, when such diverse thinkers such as Howard Gardner, focusing on mind, Daniel Goleman, focusing on emotion, and Deepak Chopra, focusing on spirit, agree about the centrality of vision to leadership. During the mid-1980s one executive asked, with more than a trace of arrogance in his voice, "Why should I tell anyone else what my vision is?" Such a question would not be asked today by any executive who attends to the literature of leadership or to how others lead. Vision became popular in the 1980s when leaders discovered that a worthwhile vision can provide purpose and focus to an organization's activities. Suddenly it seemed that every organization had to have a "vision statement" and leaders, either singly or in leadership teams, rushed off to retreat centers to craft them. That inclination continues as leaders develop statements that, sadly, more often than not are soon forgotten by those who are expected to transform them into reality.

There are many reasons for these failures. At or near the top of the list of reasons is that many visions fail to win the kind of long-term commitment that they need; their inspiration lasting only for a few days, a few weeks, or a few months.

Self or Others

Visions can be placed on a continuum from those that are *self-referent* at one end to those that are *noble* at the other. Self-referent visions are about what the organization and its people wish to become. Noble visions are about the contribution the organization's leaders wish to make to some group of people. The continuum is shown in Figure 3-1.

SELF-REFERENT VISION	NOBLE VISION
About self and/or organization	About contributing to the needs and aspirations of a group of people

Figure 3-1. Self-referent and noble vision.

Many visions, especially those crafted by corporate leaders, are self-referent. They are about the organization's business and about the leader's aspirations to dominate that business, rather than about the contribution the leaders intend to make to a group of people. A conventional corporate vision is something like this: "To be the best in the eyes of our customers, employees, and the public." This does not tell us why the organization's product or service is valuable to anyone, or how it contributes to any group of people. The vision refers only to the leader's desire to be at the helm of the best and to have everybody know it.

There is nothing wrong with being the best or having a good reputation, but such statements reflect egoistic appetites for achievement rather than contributions to the human community. Being the best can be seen as a very good idea, therefore forming the basis for intellectual commitment. It can also inspire strong emotions such as satisfaction and pride. But neither of these commitments alone is sustainable over time. Two conclusions are intuitively and experientially obvious.

1. Fundamental and sustainable great achievements, those requiring a high level of energy over a long period of time, as well as perhaps some sacrifice and pain, necessitate higher commitment than political or intellectual commitment.
2. People will offer intellectual and emotional commitment to many causes, but they will commit spiritual energy only to those visions that address the elemental needs of a group of people.

In other words, as a leader, no matter how great you wish yourself or your organization to become, if your vision only focuses on this goal, a call for a high level of commitment from others is likely to fall flat. Self-referent visions do not focus on an insight into the needs and aspirations of a group of people. Life Teen was grounded in Monsignor Fushek's insight about love. The Spiritual Eldering Institute was grounded in Rabbi Schachter-Shalomi's vision of "elderhood" as a time of contributing to society. Without a seminal insight about the needs and aspirations of a group of people, visions can easily become degraded into mere personal goals or marketing slogans. Because self-referent visions are not grounded in such insights, they fail to sustain intellectual and emotional commitment for long, and they never inspire spiritual commitment.

It is also intuitively and experientially accurate to say that the leader of an organization whose products or services do not contribute substantially to a group of people entertains false hopes when he expects high levels of commitment from employees. Self-referent visions are the last—perhaps the only—resort of leaders in such organizations.

A vision that is self-referent also casts doubt on an organization's other commitments. For example, if an organization's leaders state that they are committed to customer service, yet their vision is entirely self-referent, an onlooker might legitimately conclude that the commitment to customer service is merely political. In other words, customer service is not valued in and of itself, but as a means to another end—the organization's own achievement. This political commitment to service is the likely source of contradictory messages to customers, such as, "Your call is important to us. All of our representatives are currently busy helping other customers. Your call will be answered in twenty-two minutes." If the call truly was important, if the organization's commitment truly was to customer service rather than to its own achievement, then the call would be answered immediately.

Noble Visions

Visions that do describe a contribution to a group of people are motivated more by concern for that group rather than by personal achievement, and are most often created by leaders in social service and educational institutions. For example, Jim Wold's vision is about student performance, a hot topic and educational buzzword today, but not so well understood when he first became a school superintendent. "I didn't understand how important creating and articulating a vision was until I was a school superintendent," Jim said. He went to workshops, spoke with other superintendents, listened to tapes, read books, then asked himself, "What is the most important thing in education?" His answer was, "Improving teaching and learning so all students achieve high standards of performance." That phrase became his vision.

Today Wold says, "It really resonated with people. It was just amazing to me the focus that it helped people have; it creates a culture against which you can test everything you are doing. If it isn't about teaching and learning, and it isn't going to benefit students, than why are we doing it? I wasn't sure up to that point. I didn't know how important it was. That was a breakthrough for me. You really have to put a phrase around it to focus it."

Another example is the vision of Bloorview MacMillan Children's Centre of Ontario, Canada. Bloorview MacMillan enables children with disabilities and special needs to achieve their best. The vision is a heart stopper, "Defy Disability."[1] That's all of it: two words. It suggests a world in which disability is met head on and challenged with resolve and dignity. More importantly, it suggests that the leaders at Bloorview MacMillan care about something other than themselves. And it implies that the rest of us ought to do the same. The leadership of Bloorview MacMillan has crafted a declaration that is both a vision and a call to action.

Another noble vision comes from the leadership of Fielding Graduate Institute, which offers doctoral and master's degree programs in psychology and education. Fielding is world-renowned for innovation in higher education. It envisions, "a collaborative family of scholar-practitioners, empowered by a global perspective, enabling and promoting harmony and social justice."[2]

Noble visions such as those of Wold, Bloorview MacMillan, and Fielding Graduate Institute address the reasons that leaders do what they do (and why followers ought to do the same) beyond their own self-interest. Heather Roseveare, director of family and community relations at Bloorview MacMillan, said, "Our vision captures the heart of what we do—defy disability—but also how we do it, and why we do it."[3]

Some business leaders do pay attention to their contribution to the human community and say so when they talk about their vision. Whirlpool's leaders, for example, promote this vision: "Every Home . . . Everywhere. With Pride, Passion and Performance. We create the world's best home appliances, which make life easier and more enjoyable for all people."[4]

Yes, much of the statement is self-referent, about Whirlpool itself: about its aspiration to be everywhere, and about its values—pride, passion, and performance. But Whirlpool's leaders have also stated that making life easier and more enjoyable is their underlying reason for doing what they do. Unlike any "we want to be the best" vision, Whirlpool's leaders say that they want to be the best for a larger reason.

"We want to be the best" statements lay at the far left of the self-referent-to-noble continuum, while Whirlpool's lies in the middle, and Jim Wold's, Bloorview MacMillan's and Fielding's rest at the far right.

Two other examples of noble vision—both business examples—come from the Japanese giant NEC Corporation, where leaders have twice created visions that promise a contribution to the human community. In 1986, then Chairman Koji Kobayashi envisioned that NEC was creating "a situation that would make it possible for any person in the world to communicate with any other person at any place and any time." Then in 2001 NEC's leadership envisioned an "iSociety" in which the networks around people "promote an exchange of information and knowledge for the achievement of a new creativity in society."[5]

While noble visions such as the ones espoused by the leadership of NEC are not the corporate norm, NEC's leaders are not alone in creating such visions. The leadership of Fujita, a ninety-year-old company, which primarily does construction, planning, and design, says, "Today Fujita is rewriting history, so we can all work together to create a world that combines a rich natural environment and vibrant societies with caring communities." Fujita also states, "Our foremost aim is to enhance human happiness through achieving harmony between ecology, society, and the urban environment."[6]

"What Does the World Need?"

A story that beautifully illustrates the difference between self-referent and noble visions comes from Hewlett-Packard, which charged Barbara Waugh, a change manager, with the task of making its industrial research laboratory the best in the world. Waugh felt that somehow the vision of being the best in the world was not enough. She told the magazine *Fast Company*, "One day I'm talking about these feelings with my friend Laurie [Mitlestadt], an engineer at the lab, and she says, 'You know what I would get up for in the morning? Not to be the best *in* the world, but to be the best *for* the world.'"[7] Waugh says, "*For* the world automatically forces you to look out, not just in. It makes you ask, 'What does the world need?'"[8]

Bill Strickland understands what Waugh is getting at. He said, "A lot of the business guys say, 'My only job is to make sure that the stockholders are cool.' I say no, that is part of your job. The other part of your job is to improve the planet, make a contribution, raise some decent kids, support your fellow man, help struggling social institutions in your community. You have many jobs, one of which happens to be making money."

Strickland says of a vision such as the one Waugh describes, "It opens up the conversation and introduces a much broader agenda of items that are considered as part of our life work. We are going to lose our planet if leadership doesn't start opening up this conversation to consider more than 'me first'."

No vision, by itself, is a guarantee of success. However, noble visions such as those described above are more likely to win emotional and spiritual commitment. Most people welcome the opportunity to contribute to a group of people, a country, or the planet; to be part of some larger endeavor than "being the best."

It's Just Human Nature

Common sense suggests that self-referent visions are likely to appear when organizations really do care only for themselves, or when people in leadership positions lack either imagination or a compelling insight, or when the products and services that an organization provides truly do not make a significant contribution to any group of people (who really needs non-nutritional foods, for example). However, scholar and author Alfie Kohn suggests a more subtle and pervasive cause for self-referent visions. In his book *The Brighter Side of Human Nature*, Kohn argues persuasively that the prevailing view of human nature emphasizes its darker side at the expense of its brighter side. He wrote, "We raise our children, manage our companies, and design our governments on the assumption that people are naturally and primarily selfish and will act otherwise only if they are coerced to do so and carefully monitored."[9] This assumption provides impetus for those who hold leadership positions to settle for self-referent visions and political commitment. If people are primarily selfish, self-referent visions make sense as a way of gaining their commitment. And if they are primarily selfish, then their commitment can only be bought rather than won.

Kohn's survey of studies about people helping other people shows that the assumption is erroneous. He wrote, "People of all ages usually do go out of their way to help, particularly when the need is clear and when they believe that no one else is in a position to get involved."[10] Human beings, Kohn concludes, want to do things that benefit other people.

Bonnie Wright says it this way, "Fundamentally, people need to help other people. Look at September 11; the first reaction was not 'let's go get the guys that did this.' The first reaction was 'How can I help?'" And Pat Croce, perhaps best known as the former president of the Philadelphia 76ers basketball team, and someone we will meet in more detail in Chapter 8 said, "Too many times in our society we think that doing well has nothing to do with doing good. When you know you have done good, you will do well."

Even when groups of people or organizations care for something other than themselves, have imagination and a compelling insight, and offer products and services that do make a significant contribution to a group of people, their leaders still must guard against the assumption that human nature is inherently and primarily selfish. Those who hold leadership positions but settle for self-referent visions or political commitment may be vastly underestimating the capacity or desire of their people to commit to something noble. Bonnie Wright says this in a positive way: "Leaders help people help." In that statement she captures the essence of a leader's role in bringing a noble vision to fruition.

Vision and Identity

Visions also invite, and perhaps challenge, followers to consider both who they are now and who they aspire to become. A noble vision forces us to ask provocative questions about ourselves; about who we have been, who we are, and who we want to become. The best of these visions—those that draw the highest levels of commitment—dare us to become proud of ourselves by accomplishing something for other people.

An example of how a vision can challenge a follower's sense of who they are is found in the leadership experience of Ralph Pries. In the early 1980s, Pries became the CEO of Mediq, a six-year-old company that started by renting ventilators to hospitals and for home care. When Pries came on the scene, the company's employees variously viewed themselves as members of functional teams; they were maintenance technicians, delivery drivers, salespeople, and so forth. Pries changed that by promoting the understanding that all of their work was about "sustaining life." This new perception of their identity infused employees with a higher sense of purpose: "My work is not just about maintaining ventilators, it is about sustaining life."

Jim Wold's teachers were improving student performance. Whirlpool's technicians and sales force are making life easier and more enjoyable. The staff of Bloorview MacMillan is defying disability. Fielding

Graduate Institute's faculty and administration are creating ethical global change. NEC's people are creating the iSociety.

A manager in a company that went through a transformation similar to Mediq's said, "It is amazing how all the ridiculous things we usually do—all the turf wars, petty arguments, silly fights over resources—they all go away when everyone realizes that our work is not just about us but has some greater purpose attached to it." The primary function of vision is to enunciate and draw attention to that greater purpose.

Development Strategies for Vision

When moving from insight to vision, the danger is that the original compelling insight will suffer, becoming less compelling and less an instrument for attracting commitment. Because of this danger, leaders must pay careful attention to the process of crafting a vision, and must carefully consider the choices they make about this process and about their own roles within it. Leaders typically take one of four roles in relation to a vision; they may articulate the vision themselves, or steer a vision-making process that involves other people, or allow a vision to emerge naturally, or adopt someone else's vision. Each of these roles places different demands on a leader.

Articulating a Vision Yourself

When leaders articulate a vision themselves, their work then becomes communicating it in such a way that it draws commitment from others. This is the model that we most often think of as the true expression of leadership. The strength of this model is that, the leader will invariably stand as the primary spokesperson and symbol for the vision, whether she likes it or not, and so it is imperative that she take full ownership for it. The weakness of this model is that leaders must eventually be inclusive, and involving people to create what will become their vision is one way to begin winning their commitment.

Steering a Group Process

When a leader chooses to participate in a vision-making process with other people, he opens up the possibility for those others to also take ownership of the vision. Lieutenant General Jim Ellis, talking about his earliest lessons in leadership, discovered the value of such an approach. Ellis entered West Point from the ranks of the enlisted, graduated, and later taught there as an Assistant Professor of International Relations and Economics. During his career he commanded The Third Army (Patton's Own) and served as Deputy Commander-in-Chief of the U.S. Central Command. After a thirty-nine year career, Ellis retired in 1994 with over forty awards, including three Distinguished Service Medals. He then became executive director and CEO of The Boggy Creek Gang Camp, one of many such camps sponsored by Paul Newman, which each year serves thousands of children suffering from chronic and life threatening illnesses. Ellis is also a senior vice president of Endur, Inc.

Very early in his military career, Ellis was called upon do be the aide-de-camp of the new commanding general of the 82nd Airborne Division. Ellis said, "He came in at a time when the division had been in flux. We had had some organizational changes with some pretty demanding things from on high that had kept us in an uproar. When the old commander went out there was a lot of confusion." The new commanding general insisted on asking, "What are we all about? What are the vision and mission, goals and objectives of this organization," said Ellis. "He made everybody stop and think instead of running around. He made us focus on the purpose of the organization. That settled things down and gave people a definition of where to go."

Ellis continued, "He gave us a chance to reflect in a collective atmosphere with all of his chief subordinates. He accepted input from many, many people, including the higher headquarters. He gave us an azimuth and a path. It was incredibly successful and it shaped the future of the division for quite a long time."

When leaders choose to steer a vision-making process that involves others in creating the vision, as Ellis' commanding general did, their work becomes facilitating that process while at the same time holding onto their own insight and making certain that the final vision expresses it. The strength of this model is that it is more inclusive from the beginning, drawing higher commitment earlier from people whose commitment will eventually be needed. The weakness of this model is that in the attempt to be inclusive, the vision becomes subject to whatever dynamics pervade the group charged with articulating it. Groups creating visions often try to reach a synthesis of ideas and end up with something that satisfies everybody but excites nobody.

Kathy Covert says of such efforts, "They lose the juice." Covert is Secretary of the GeoData Alliance, an organization she founded to bring together individuals and institutions committed to using geographic information to improve human communities. She also serves on several nonprofit boards and, most notably for a discussion of leadership, she is on the Council of Trustees of the Chaordic Commons. This organization seeks to develop and share new concepts about human organizations. In tune with her interest in improving human communities and organizations, she is very thoughtful about her own leadership role.

Covert has been through enough unsatisfying experiences with groups trying to create a vision statement that she is wary of the process. "People don't realize when a vision doesn't resonate," she said. In her experience, the process of synthesizing the varied ideas of a group of people in order to create a vision statement that eventually satisfies everybody but excites nobody leads to the adoption of a vision because of the, "Horror of opening it up again."

A group that insists everyone be fully satisfied will create a catch-all vision; a group that cannot reach the deepest levels of their humanity will produce a watered-down vision; a group that has competitive desires raging among its members will produce a self-referent vision. Also, a group that thrives on intellect will produce a vision that is likely to attract intellectual commitment, one that thrives on emotion is likely to produce a vision that will attract emotional commitment, and one that thrives on spirit is likely to produce a vision that will attract spiritual commitment. Any leader who proposes to have a group create a vision is well advised to ensure that the group has developed a constructive way of working together, and that its members have competence to win high levels of commitment, before being given this most important task.

Jim Ellis also offers a word of caution to leaders who walk into leadership positions where the organization and people are already in place and the work is ongoing, as was the case when he was aide-de-camp to the commanding general of the 82nd Airborne Division. In these situations steering a process that results in a vision takes courage. "It is awfully easy to roll with the tide," Ellis said, "Instead of taking the hard course of stepping back and taking a look and asking, 'Are we really doing the right things? Are we achieving to the best of our abilities what it is this organization is supposed to achieve?'"

Another word of caution was expressed by Mary Ellen Hennen, who we will meet in more detail in Chapter 8. Hennen said that her own visions of the future have been with her for so long and are so much a part of who she is that, "I don't see it anymore." She knows the principles that drive her own leadership so well—they come so naturally to her— that working through a vision-making process with a group of people can become tedious, and she can easily tune out.

As Jim Ellis learned from the commanding general of the 82nd Airborne Division, an inclusive vision-making process can have great benefit. It is also fraught with peril.

Allowing a Vision to Emerge

Leaders choosing to allow a vision to emerge naturally must be attentive to opportunities that will enable them to continue to act on their original insight and respond to these opportunities. This is what Monsignor Fushek did after Life Teen was successful in his own parish. He responded to calls from other parishes, helping them to replicate his success. He guided the fledgling organization to develop a training package for other parishes and to present training conferences nationwide. He did not articulate a vision.

Fushek's approach makes sense to Michael Jones, who said, "I have had a real struggle trying to figure out how vision fits in. Vision seems to me to include a path of certainty that cuts you off from the very process of creation that helps accomplish great things."

The advantage of allowing a vision to emerge naturally and to remain a fluid thing is that the potential for creative responses to threats and opportunities is higher. The disadvantage is that the process may leave those who seek certainty and who are uncomfortable with ambiguity feeling adrift and rudderless. Many leaders articulate a vision only because they are expected to, or because it has utility as a bridge between their insight and the commitment of others.

Adopting a Vision

When leaders take on someone else's vision, their work becomes making it their own, and expressing it in ways that are both faithful to the original and to their own insights. This was the course taken by Dawn Gutierrez, who is executive director of New Way Learning Academy, a school whose mission is to serve children with learning disabilities and attention deficit disorders, as well as children who are underachievers. New Way had been operating for twenty-five years when Gutierrez took over in 1993. With her leadership, New Way has doubled its enrollment, nearly tripled its staff, increased the depth of the programs it offers, greatly developed its teacher training, added technology, purchased its own building, and significantly improved its business operations.

Gutierrez had been a teacher at New Way for five years. Its founders were near retirement when she asked them what her future might be at the school. They recognized Gutierrez' leadership potential, saw her as someone who could carry on their work, offered her the executive director's job, and agreed to mentor her as she grew as a leader. She says, "First of all I had to believe in their mission. I bought into it right away. I think I was able to do that because I already had an experience in the public setting and saw what could be done through a private nonprofit school. I already had it. When I found New Way I didn't have any problem continuing with the founders' mission."

No matter which of these four courses a leader chooses, his vision must be worthy of the commitment of other people; it must attract that commitment. And no matter which of these courses a leader chooses, he must be prepared to be its primary spokesperson and primary symbol.

Summary

A vision serves as a statement about how a leader intends to create concrete reality out of her insight. Visions that have a noble rather than a self-referent quality are far more likely to win the commitment of others and to provide followers with a noble sense of who they are and who they are becoming. A leader can take a variety of roles in articulating a vision.

· · ·

Questions About Yourself to Contemplate or Discuss with Others

Who, in your life experience, was practiced at vision?

To what degree are you practiced at vision?

What is it about vision that rings true for your current leadership role?

How important is vision to your further development as a leader?

Notes

1. Bloorview-Macmillan Children's Center, "Our Vision, Values, and Mission," <http://www.bloorviewmacmillan.on.ca/webpdfs/visvalmis.pdf> (January, 2002).
2. Fielding Graduate Institute, <http://www.fielding.edu> (January, 2002).
3. Dick Richards, *Worthy Visions Pass One Simple Test* (Louisville, Ky.: BrownHerron Publishing, 2002). <www.amazon.com/brownherron>.
4. Whirlpool Corp, "Every Home . . . Everywhere," <http://www.whirlpoolcorp.com/whr/corporate/vision.html> (January, 2003).
5. NEC Corporation, "Report on NEC's Third Environmental Forum 2001," <http://www.nec.co.jp/eco/en/forum2001/future/> (January, 2003).

6. Fujita, "About Fujita Corporation," <http://www.fujita.com/index2.html> (January, 2003).
7. Polly LaBarre, "Attitude Adjustment," *Fast Company* (October, 2001): 46.
8. Mark Albion, "Take the Brand Challenge," <http://www.fastcompany.com/career/albion/0100.html> (January, 2003).
9. Alfie Kohn, *The Brighter Side of Human Nature*, (N.Y.: Basic Books, 1990): 4.
10. Ibid, 64.

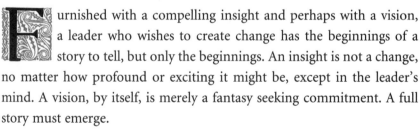

4

Storytelling

Experience is not what happens to you; it's what you do with what happens to you.

—ALDOUS HUXLEY

urnished with a compelling insight and perhaps with a vision, a leader who wishes to create change has the beginnings of a story to tell, but only the beginnings. An insight is not a change, no matter how profound or exciting it might be, except in the leader's mind. A vision, by itself, is merely a fantasy seeking commitment. A full story must emerge.

For his book *Leading Minds*, Howard Gardner studied in depth the lives and work of eleven leaders, including such diverse people as Alfred P. Sloan Jr., Pope John XXIII, Margaret Thatcher, and Mohandas Gandhi. Gardner says of the eleven leaders:

They told stories—in so many words—about themselves and their groups, about where they were coming from and where they were headed, about what was to be feared, struggled against, and dreamed about.[1]

Gardner also explains that leaders do not so much *tell* a story as *relate* it through their day-to-day actions, their histories, and the kinds of lives they lead. Gardner summarizes this point straightforwardly: "People who do not practice what they preach are hypocrites, and hypocrisy mutes the effectiveness of their stories."[2] It has become a cliché, but is nonetheless true—leaders must "walk the talk." They win intellectual commitment through their insight and vision, through congruence between what they say and what they do, and through a life that embodies the change they espouse. Taken together, these are the ingredients of a leader's story, and the basis of a leader's influence. Because today's world is one of instantaneous communication and multiple channels of communication, a leader's ability to tell a story has never been more central to his ability to win commitment.

Storyteller Annette Simmons wrote, "When you want to influence others, there is no tool more powerful than story." A good story, she says, forms a mental imprint that can touch others at many levels: "As a storyteller you borrow a story's power to connect people to what is important and to help them make sense of their world."[3]

The stories leaders tell contain three narrative threads:

1. A personal narrative
2. A narrative about a quest for change
3. A narrative of identity

These threads intertwine like separate plotlines in a tightly woven novel. Remove any one of them and the story unravels; it no longer makes sense and is unlikely to evoke commitment. But the full story can have great power, especially when told in an unforgettable way.

The Personal Narrative

A leader's personal narrative contains both her life story and who she is as a person. Monsignor Dale Fushek learned about the importance of his own personal narrative from Mother Teresa when, in 1989, she visited Phoenix, Arizona, where Fushek lives and works. She was in Phoenix to dedicate a homeless shelter. At the end of a busy day she told him, "People gave me some money to help start the home here. Would you take it and put it in the bank?" The diminutive nun then reached in her pockets again and again, extracting cash and checks, and handing it all over to Fushek. He stuffed it into his own pockets. When he got home that night, he emptied his pockets and counted the money. There was over $33,000—all of it money that people had handed to her during the course of that one day. It was not lost on Fushek that he had been with her all day and people had not handed $33,000 to him.

When asked what meaning this experience had for him, Fushek said, "People don't give to things, they give to people. They want to be part of something in some way through someone who can help them be more than they feel they can be on their own." When he spoke of people giving, it was clear that he was speaking not only about money, but also about time and energy; he was speaking about commitment. People commit to leaders who relate compelling stories and who live lives that are congruent with their stories.

Wilma Mankiller is a very good example of a leader whose life and work, insight and vision, and congruence between what she says and does, together form just such a compelling story. She was the first woman to be elected chief of the Cherokee Nation. She held the position for ten years, winning her second term in 1991 with 83 percent of the vote. Later, after voluntarily relinquishing her role as chief because of ill health, Mankiller emerged as a leader in the fight against stereotyping and prejudice: in particular, against stereotypes and prejudices about Native Americans and about women. She does so from the platform of a life of personal battles against those who stereotyped her and held prejudice toward her—both as a Native American and as a woman. For example, during the period when she was campaigning to become leader of the Cherokee Nation many tribal members asked her to withdraw. She received hate mail and threatening phone calls, and endured the slashing of her tires and death threats. The suggestion of a woman as chief was not universally popular within the tribe, some claiming that it offended God.[4]

During her ten years as chief, the Cherokee Nation's annual budget was more than $75 million dollars. Mankiller oversaw more than 1,200 employees. She was named *Ms. Magazine*'s "Woman of the Year" in 1987, was honored with a Chubb Fellowship from Yale University in 1995, and was awarded the Presidential Medal of Freedom in 1998.[5]

In a speech at Sweet Briar College in 1993, Mankiller said, "If we are ever going to collectively begin to grapple with the problems that we have collectively, we are going to have to move back the veil and deal with each other on a more human level."[6] The "veil" that she speaks of is created by stereotypes and misunderstandings that prevent people from communicating with one another in a meaningful way. Her call for people of all kinds to relate to one another on a more human level, and to turn their backs on stereotyping and prejudice, clearly reflects her own battles with being typecast as a Native American and as a woman.

There is also a subterranean echo lurking in her leadership. Her entreaty for respect and interconnectedness among the world's various peoples reflects her Native American understanding of human relationships. She says, "I was brought up in a Cherokee community where it was implicitly understood that we are responsible for one other, that we survive in reciprocal relationships."

The words she speaks and the music of her life fit together; everything supports everything else in a highly congruent way—there are no false notes. She sings the kind of song that attracts commitment. Her friend, publisher and writer Gloria Steinem, says of her, "I think, if this country had any sense, Wilma would be president."[7]

This congruence between what a leader says, who that leader is as a person, and how that leader lives her life, is important for three reasons. First, a leader's personal narrative establishes her credibility and helps followers answer the basic questions any follower will ask: *Who is this person? Can he be trusted? Can he help me and others transcend our current circumstances?* People were charitable with Mother Teresa because she was charitable toward others. People listen to Wilma Mankiller's plea to be responsible for one another because she was raised in and reflects a culture that embodies such values. She carries her convictions with her everywhere she goes, establishing her authority when she speaks about them.

The second reason that congruence between a leader's words and life is important is that leaders are human and will inevitably do something that seems incongruent, or off purpose, or out of character. Also, even when leaders believe they are being totally consistent, their actions will sometimes appear inconsistent to others. And, those around them may act in a leader's name in ways that are inconsistent with the overall message. It is inevitable that a leader will be seen as singing out of tune. A leader who consciously and constantly tells her own personal story will accumulate the trust needed to overcome these gaffs and misunderstandings. When incongruity or its appearance does show up, followers who have heard the story from the leader's own lips, are more likely to ask, *"What is going on?"* rather than to make the immediate assumption that the leader has strayed off course or is oblivious to her impact.

The third reason that a leader's personal narrative is important to her story is that leaders cannot expect higher commitment than they themselves have given. A leader's personal narrative explains why she has made a commitment and what that commitment entails. So, when a leader whose personal story is well-known asks for commitment from others, those who are being asked know that the person who is asking understands what the request means; actions and consequences, struggles and sacrifices, pain and joy—all of it. In a very real sense, leaders say to followers, "Come and share my life." That invitation is offered through the telling of the leader's personal narrative.

General Jim Ellis summarized the importance of the leader's personal narrative when he said, "The leader as an individual will inspire other people just because of who he is and the way he lives his life as an individual and as a leader. How wonderful would it be if you were known through your life as 'Honest Abe?' How much could you do? Wouldn't that be amazing, to have that reputation?"

The Quest for Change

Leaders also serve as narrators for the unfolding drama that is any change process. They keep the original insight or vision firmly in the forefront of their own awareness and the minds of their followers, and also remind followers about where their quest began. Bonnie Wright said, "I wasn't afraid to go back to the beginning over, and over, and over again. 'Remember when we said we were going to do *this*. Remember we agreed on *this*.' Because people don't remember." Wright's continual returning to the beginning is not merely a matter of reminding people about what they had agreed to. It is also about returning to what holds the group together. "Always go back to common ground," she said.

Leaders also comment in both words and actions about the progress of their mutual pursuit. They give updates about what has happened, what is happening, and what must happen next. They become the keepers of the story. For example, in 1947, after India had achieved independence from Britain, Hindus and Muslims fought violently with one another in riots across the country. Mohandas Gandhi fasted, and promised to continue fasting until the violence came to an end. This was Gandhi's very live and very dramatic update about what India had hoped to achieve for itself, about the problems within India that threatened the peace and stability of the recently created nation. Gandhi's fast was a potent reminder that there was work yet to be accomplished. It reminded Indians of where they had been, where they were, where they wanted to be, and what they needed to do next.

A leader's function as the narrator of the change process is to maintain the creative tension required to keep commitment flowing. That tension results from the gap between where people are and where they want to be. That gap can be an unsettling place—a tense place. The leader's job is to make sure people know that they are indeed in a tense place.

The tension can become a source of energy to move forward. Gandhi's fast was, in effect, a statement that went something like this: "Hold on now. We have made progress but we aren't there yet. And we'll never get there unless you all stop beating up on one another." Gandhi delivered that message in a way that assured it would not be missed.

A Narrative of Identity

The third narrative that is woven into a leader's story is about the identity of followers. Among the reasons followers offer commitment to leaders are their aspirations to become somehow, in some way, better people. Of his encounter with Mother Teresa, Monsignor Fushek now says, "I realized, not in any way with ego, that if I was going to do anything that was going to make a difference, I had to help people to become better than they thought they could become on their own." And Gloria Steinem said of Wilma Mankiller, "She makes each of us a little better than we would otherwise be."[8]

Sometimes a leader's narrative about the identity of followers draws upon and reinforces deeply held beliefs about who they are. For example, Wilma Mankiller, true to Cherokee beliefs about people taking care of one another, promised to build primary health care clinics in two rural communities. Cherokee people clearly stated that they wanted medical care closer to their communities. She committed to obtain funding to build two new clinics. It took ten years of lobbying Congress, and a seemingly endless series of meetings and justifications to Indian Health Service officials, to obtain funding to build the clinics.

At other times, a leader's narrative about the identity of followers challenges their perceptions about themselves, impelling them to become better by becoming different than they are. For example, Margaret Thatcher's narrative of identity was based on creating a society in which individual initiative and choice won out over the restraints imposed by the massive state apparatus that characterized Britain before she was elected Prime Minister.

Three Unforgettable Stories

Telling a compelling story requires much more than facility with words, graphs, numbers, and logic. It also requires a sense of drama that is too often missing in attempts to exert leadership. Business people recognize this scene: An executive of the company stands before them at a podium in a semidarkened room going over a PowerPoint presentation about a new company vision, mission, or strategy. The reaction of the audience ranges between polite attention and glazed eyes. At the end of the presentation, the words, "Any questions?" are met first with an awkward silence, then with a prudent question or two that draw a long and detailed response producing more polite attention and glazed eyes. When the questioning ends, the executive gives a brief pep talk and the audience applauds. Then everybody leaves with no greater commitment to anything, and nothing changes very much.

Here are three examples of stories dramatically told:

1. An executive who headed a product line division of a petrochemical firm asked his senior managers to attend a meeting at a seaside resort. The division was in serious trouble and he knew that business as usual would not solve their problems. The managers arrived with their presentations and handouts as they always did. They were well prepared to report to him and to their peers about the progress of projects, about financial results and projections, and about opportunities and challenges. They expected each would have a turn at a lectern, but as they arrived he invited them to join him on the beach and to bring all of their material. The charts, graphs, and handouts were set ablaze in a bonfire. When the flames settled he said, "Now let's go inside and talk honestly to one another about what we must do."

2. Nobel Laureate physicist Richard Feynman testified before a congressional committee investigating the *Challenger* disaster. In the days immediately following the tragedy, most engineers close to the investigation were convinced that the explosion of the *Challenger* resulted from the failure of a rubber seal—an "o-ring"—on one of *Challenger*'s

booster rockets. Those who ascribed to this theory believed that the failure of the seal was caused by low temperature at the time of the launch. But blame was cast in many directions and the facts were murky. During his testimony, Feynman placed a section of an o-ring in a clamp, tightened it, and dropped this construction into a glass of ice water. Explaining his point as the rubber became colder, he then removed the clamp and produced a section of o-ring that was transformed by the cold from flexible to hard and inflexible. Anyone who was at the hearing, or who read the front page the next day, understood what happened to *Challenger*.

3. A woman was promoted to become senior vice president for the human relations function of a large corporation. One of her most immediate tasks was to appoint two new members of her management team. During her first speech to the entire human resources group she announced her appointments. Many in the audience were surprised by her choices. Then she explained, "I talked to the people we serve—to our internal customers and partners. I asked them who among us provides them with the best service. I made these two promotions based on what they told me."

The messages in these three examples were unmistakable: We need to learn to talk honestly with one another, an o-ring failed, serving our customers will be rewarded. Furthermore, the messages were delivered in ways that are unforgettable. The ability to deliver unmistakable messages in unforgettable ways is the art of storytelling.

Development Strategies for Storytelling

The *New York Times* called Odds Bodkin "a consummate storyteller." He has mesmerized audiences at Lincoln Center, the White House, schools, universities, museums, and theaters across America. He has also created seventeen award-winning audio recordings. Bodkin offers four pieces of advice for leaders who wish to become better storytellers: exercise your imagination, rely on imagery, risk being a person, and become conversant with mythology.

Exercising Imagination

"Human imagination is almost an ecological force," says Bodkin, "What we imagine tends much more to become what actually happens than what we don't imagine." Bodkin urges people to discover the *Five Imaginations*, each connected to one of the five senses: sight, hearing, touch, smell, and taste. He says, "If you learn to use them simultaneously, that thing that you are imagining inside yourself, that you want to get out and share with others, becomes incredibly vivid." He asks, "Can you imagine the aroma of a freshly cut orange?" If you can, you are using one of the Five Imaginations. Imagination, says Bodkin, is like a muscle—you have to exercise it.[9]

Leaders ask people to imagine the future. That imagining will be much more vivid if people become aware of their five senses and use their Five Imaginations. Bodkin says, "It gives you a lot of avenues toward expressing what you want to express, and will personalize it and almost automatically take you into the place of how to say, 'Look. I am a human being. I am trying to do this in the world. You are human beings and we are trying to do this together. And above and beyond all the rest of our activities, be they technological, actuarial, or whatever, we are all in this together.'"

Relying on Imagery

Once leaders have exercised their Five Imaginations, they are prepared to stimulate vivid images in the imaginations of others. Bodkin uses an image of his own to illustrate the point. He suggests imagining an hourglass tilted on its side. The narrow neck of the hourglass is for communication between the two halves. There is a huge sphere, the leader's imagination, on one side. The leader's task is to make the other sphere the same. He says, "To get one sphere to resemble the other—the little neck where the sand moves through—that is the story time. It has to be pretty good otherwise one sphere will be this immense round glorious thing, and the other will be a little bulb—people won't be getting it."

If Bodkin were here now, he would have us go beyond merely imagining how his hourglass looks, and perhaps imagining the whisper of sand moving through the hourglass, the musty smell of an antique timepiece, or the feel of smooth glass under our hands.

Risking Being a Person

Bodkin says, "I never work from a script but from mental imagery." He goes before an audience with a series of pictures in his mind. His job is to help that audience imagine the pictures. "It is really best when it is extemporaneous," he says. "People instantly know that. They pick that up like electricity. They say, wow, this person is creating before my eyes. People immediately understand that means the person speaking to them has thought a heck of a lot about what they are doing, more so than the person who has a script."

In order to do this, he says, one must, "Risk being a person."

Becoming Conversant with Myth

Bodkin also says, "Being conversant with myths is a handy thing, especially for leaders." Myths can enlighten us about our circumstances, about ourselves as individuals and as members of the human race, and about who we might become. Leaders can inform themselves about their own circumstances, and also inspire people at a deep level of the psyche, when they choose the right mythical stories as metaphors for their own stories.

As an example he uses a story from the *Odyssey*. Odysseus has left the island of Circe. She has warned him that he will have to pass through the Strait of Scylla and Charybdis, where a huge six-headed dragon lurks on the left and a giant whirlpool that will destroy his ship lies on the right. Here is a leader who is between a rock and a hard place. Circe has pointed out to Odysseus that, whatever course he chooses, at least six of his men will die—prey to the six-headed dragon. If he does not stay to the left of the strait, within the dragon's reach, everyone will die in the whirlpool.

Bodkin says, "This is a story about downsizing." There is great power in telling such stories in order to illustrate and examine the challenges faced by a leader and his followers. He says, "When an archetypal instance occurs you feel this rush of identity. It is as if the whole human race resounds within you."

Using Every Point of Contact

Every point of contact between a leader and her followers or potential followers is a storytelling opportunity, and a story emerges from every contact, whether the leader wishes it to or not. It is imperative, then, that leaders consciously make use of all the storytelling opportunities they have—the rich variety of channels available to tell their stories. For example, Dale Fushek's Life Teen organization helps teens embark on their own journey of faith with special teen masses, a Web site, and retreats, and helps parishes across the globe start their own chapters with informational and training materials.

Beginning in the Comfort Zone

Sometimes it helps for a leader to begin telling his story in a way that is comfortable and familiar. For example, the CEO of a midsize company was an introverted man who preferred to communicate with his people in writing. He wrote regularly for the company newsletter and sent frequent e-mail bulletins. Writing gave him the time to think through what he wanted to say, and to make certain (at least in his own mind) that he had covered all the bases. He was very personable and likeable in one-on-one discussions and in small casual groups, but uncomfortable at a dais. When his organization was faced with a dramatic change in focus it became necessary for him to be more visible—to tell his story more widely and to be more accessible. His name was Bob.

The human resources manager for the company found a coach who would help Bob with his presentation skills. She also suggested a series of "Lunch with Bob" meetings. Once a week, Bob met with a half-dozen randomly chosen employees for lunch in a corner of the company cafeteria, visible to everyone who was there at the time. They talked about the business in general, about needed change, about his vision and hopes, and about their anxieties and questions. People sometimes wandered over to listen in and ask questions. "Lunch with Bob" was a big hit!

Summary

The telling of a leader's story is an absolute requirement for winning intellectual commitment. When leaders have stories to tell that build on their insights and visions, when they tell their stories through words and fitting actions, when their stories are about their own lives, the character of their followers, and a quest for change, when the stories serve to maintain the creative tension of the moment, and when the stories are told in memorable ways, then they can win intellectual commitment. In addition, a well-told story can also win emotional and spiritual commitment when the leader has mastered the competencies to do so. A well-told story can resonate at all levels in those that hear it.

· · ·

Questions About Yourself to Contemplate or Discuss with Others

Who, in your life experience, was practiced at storytelling?

To what degree are you practiced at storytelling?

What is it about storytelling that rings true for your current leadership role?

How important is storytelling to your further development as a leader?

Notes

1. Howard Gardner, *Leading Minds: An Anatomy of Leadership* (N.Y.: Basic Books, 1995): 14.
2. Ibid, 9.
3. Annette Simmons, *The Story Factor: Secrets of Influence from the Art of Storytelling* (Cambridge, Mass.: Perseus Publishing, 2001): 29.
4. Wilma Mankiller and Michael Wallis, *Mankiller: A Chief and Her People* (N.Y.: St. Martin's Press, 1993): 239–241.
5. Historical background about Wilma Mankiller was derived from her book *Mankiller: A Chief and Her People*. Also from Charles T. Jones, "Wilma's Spirit Survives Adversity," *The Cherokee Observer* (August 1999), and from Andrew Nelson, "Brilliant Careers: Wilma Mankiller," at <http://www.buzzle.com> (November 20, 2001).
6. "Rebuilding the Cherokee Nation," speech by Wilma Mankiller at Sweet Briar College (April 2, 1993). Source, <http://gos.sbc.edu/m/mankiller.html>.
7. Jones, "Wilma's Spirit Survives Adversity."
8. Jones, "Wilma's Spirit Survives Adversity."
9. <http://www.oddsbodkin.com/ArchivedKidsArticles.htm>.

5

Mobilizing

Even if you're on the right track, you'll get run over if you just sit there.

—WILL ROGERS

A great story that is well told creates energy within those who hear it. If that story is cogent and unforgettable, that energy can be transformed into intellectual commitment. If it is also uplifting and human and challenges people to pursue a noble vision, it can win emotional and spiritual commitment as well—if the leader has the competence to tell the story well.

But the mere telling of the story is not enough. Leaders must capture and direct the energy that the story creates—they must mobilize it. Leaders have four important responsibilities to perform in order to mobilize the energy their stories create. Fulfilling these responsibilities transforms the energy into committed action. The responsibilities are:

1. Enrolling people
2. Educating them
3. Helping them to narrow the broader challenges of an insight or a vision into actions they can perform
4. Doing all of the above in a way that conveys trust, respect, and optimism, and that invites emotional and spiritual commitment as well as intellectual commitment

The Last Five Percent

Marvin Israelow learned about the need to mobilize the energy of others, and it was a thorny lesson. In the middle of the 1980s, Israelow, with his wife Dorian and their three school-age sons, moved from midtown Manhattan to upstate Chappaqua, New York. They moved there partly because of the schools, which are consistently rated among the best in the United States. Israelow, with much experience at helping to develop businesses both large and small, and with some experience in education, knew that he had something to contribute to the Chappaqua School District. An opportunity arose because Chappaqua was searching for a new superintendent of schools. Israelow received an invitation to serve on a task force that was creating long-term goals for the school district as a way of giving direction to the new superintendent.

While serving on the task force Israelow began to see the danger that lurked beneath Chappaqua's reputation for superior education. He says, "The school district had become complacent as a result of a lot of people from across the country having come to pat it on its back. I knew from my experience as a consultant that this was a death knell for an organization."

Israelow decided he would seek more formal leadership responsibility, with more authority and influence. He ran for a seat on the school board on a platform against complacency and in favor of continuous improvement. Israelow lost the election.

"I had a well-honed message," he says, "And I believed that simply by having a message that spoke truth, the message itself would be sufficient to get me elected."

Israelow did not let defeat deter him. He felt committed, felt a sense of urgency, and also felt some personal calling to do the job he had sought. He says, "I had the experience of being in a place at a time with certain knowledge and a set of skills. All of that coalesced. It pulled me to move the district from where it was to a place that I was inspired to know that it was supposed to be." Even though it was somewhat humiliating to be defeated in his first public election, he tried again. Israelow says, "Although I had grand broad vision and I had the right message, the right concept of a change that was needed, what I hadn't done was pay enough attention to mobilizing people. I had to do the last 5 percent that needs to get done to take an idea and a leadership initiative to fruition."

For his second try at election to the School Board, Israelow knew he would need about a thousand votes to be successful. He enrolled 50 people to be his messengers. Each of them committed to enrolling 20 additional people, making sure they went to the polls and voted for him. This time he won, and he later served a term as the School Board's president.

There are situations where the full flowering of leadership seems to come unbidden, where commitment is offered when it was not actively sought. For example, after Monsignor Fushek had initial success with Life Teen in his own parish, other parishes sought his help. And Rabbi Schachter-Shalomi states that his leadership came to him as a result of ideas he put forth. But in situations such as Israelow's, where followers are actively sought, the importance of some type of formal enrollment process cannot be overstated. For Israelow, that process involved enrolling 50 people to get voters to the polls.

Always Educating

Another leadership responsibility in mobilizing the energy of followers, beyond enrolling them, is that of educating them. It is a responsibility that David Hollister understands well because he was a high school teacher before embarking on his distinguished political career. During his tenure as a state representative of Michigan, Hollister sponsored the first mandatory seat belt law in the United States. He had research showing that mandatory seat belts would save lives, would reduce both the number and the severity of injuries, and would result in saving Medicaid dollars. However, other research showed that 65 percent of the people polled about mandatory seat belts opposed the idea.

Hollister says, "It was going to be a political nightmare because public opinion was against me." Hollister undertook a campaign to change public opinion; it lasted almost four years. The bill finally won passage. He now says that, as a leader, "You are always building a base. You are always educating." This kind of education acknowledges that people are far more likely to act on their own conclusions than they are on someone else's. Mere *telling* is not enough—the key is education that allows people to draw their own conclusions.

Sometimes the education process takes longer. Hollister also worked to enact power of attorney legislation that would allow people to designate another person to make health care decisions for them if they were ever incapacitated and unable make those decisions for themselves. When he began his bid to enact the legislation, he said, "We did some polling and I knew it was going to be a loser." It took sixteen years to get the legislation passed by the Michigan legislature. "I knew that going in," says Hollister. "This is very complicated. It is going to take time. So anything that we did (during those sixteen years) had to have a public education strategy. You educate on the process, on the vision, on implementation strategies, or on how to build partnerships."

Narrowing the Challenge

The third leadership responsibility in mobilizing followers is helping them to narrow the challenges of the initial insight or vision into actions they can and will perform. Those who offer intellectual commitment to a leader may be slow to act, or may not act at all. Those who offer emotional commitment will act, but may be off purpose. Those who are spiritually committed may chafe at the inevitable barriers that confront any change, no matter how worthwhile the change may be. This third responsibility involves helping followers find an answer to the question, "How can I best contribute?"

For example, when David Hollister wanted to enact new legislation requiring mandatory seat belts, the Michigan State Police were supportive. They added a check box to their fatal accident form to indicate whether those killed had been wearing seat belts. The data they collected helped convince the public that the legislation was needed. And Marvin Israelow's fifty messengers had a very practical and specific role to perform—get twenty voters to the polls to vote for him.

Jim Ellis talked about how he learned the important lesson that leaders have a responsibility to help their followers know exactly how to contribute. "I was a private," Ellis said, "My sergeant made it his job to train me and to treat me with dignity and respect even though I was an eighteen year old who really didn't know a whole lot. He showed me what could be done, what I could do, and how I could respond and do the things that were necessary for me to succeed in my role."

Ellis asks, "Have you ever known anybody who gets up in the morning saying, 'By God, today I'm going to screw up?'" Ellis is absolutely convinced that everybody in an organization wants to do the right thing. He says, "What is important for the leader is making sure that the follower who wants to do well knows what doing well means. Maybe what he thinks is doing well is not really good for the organization."

Former U.S. Army General Wesley Clark echoes Ellis's words when talking about the dramatic shift from an army that was essentially coercive in nature to one that is built upon the voluntary participation of its members. Clark is best known as the former commander-in-chief, U.S. European Command, who led the military negotiations for the Bosnian Peace Accords at Dayton, and as a CNN military analyst. Clark called the transformation of the U.S. army into a volunteer force "a wholesale turnaround" in which the discipline through which soldiers learned their jobs came to be viewed as a positive force. "It is like the discipline you have for a football line," said Clark. "Hey. Don't jump offside. It's not like we are just trying to keep you from jumping offside, it is because that is the way you play the game. If you want to win, you don't get a penalty." The challenge—the military objective of the moment—becomes narrowed to specific actions that are performed well.

Helping people to narrow the challenge means ensuring that every group of people involved (and eventually every person), understands how its work contributes to the overall effort. This may mean reprioritizing a group's activities, it may mean starting new activities, and it may mean stopping activities that do not contribute. Organizational leaders who seek change must pay conscious and deliberate attention to making sure this reprioritizing, starting, and stopping of activities actually happens. Leaders are in danger when they assume that people will know what to do differently because they have heard the story and gotten the message. That assumption is a genuine vision-killer.

Thinking Together

The processes of enrolling and educating followers, and helping them to find their own ways to contribute, entails an ongoing relationship between leaders and their followers. This relationship has been described in many ways, but there is general agreement among leaders and those who theorize about leadership that mutual learning is at the center of the relationship. Gardner, for example, says that the relationship is one in which, "Each takes cues from the other; each is affected by the other."[1] And Chopra says that followers and their needs, and leaders and their responses, cocreate each other.[2]

The cocreation that Chopra refers to occurs through an extended and evocative dialogue between a leader and followers. The common understanding of the term *dialogue*—a simple talk between people—does not approach the meaning of the term as it is intended here. The kind of dialogue that forms the bond between a leader and followers more closely resembles the meaning of dialogue as it is described by David Bohm, who is often hailed as one of the greatest physicists and thinkers of the twentieth century. Bohm turned his attention to human communication during the later years of his life. He viewed dialogue as an exchange, involving any number of people, which makes possible "a flow of meaning in the whole group." It is characterized by a spirit of attempting to create a new understanding within the group that may in turn lead to new ways of acting.[3]

Dialogue of this kind is not a mere exchange of information and opinion. No one is attempting to win or score points. It is not mere discussion, nor is it argumentation, debate, or a speech followed by a question-and-answer session; although each of these things might, in their own way, be useful. It is, rather, a mutual inquiry, perhaps extending over a long period of time. The inquiry utilizes all of the information— including intellectual, emotional, and spiritual information—that the participants bring to the dialogue. The kind of dialogue that Bohm describes is sometimes referred to as *collective thinking* or *thinking together*.[4]

While Bohm's dialogue is based on the use of language, the content of the dialogue between a leader and followers includes everything the leader does and says, everything followers do and say, and their respective reactions to what each other does and says. When all of these words, actions, and reactions are employed in the service of mutual learning, we have a kind of dialogue. It is less a technique or a well-defined process than it is an attitude of mutual learning that pervades how leaders and followers treat the messages they offer to and receive from one another.

Marvin Isrealow's dialogue with the community in which he would eventually assume a leadership role began when he was a relative newcomer to Chappaqua, several years before his successful bid for election. He volunteered to serve on the committee that was charged with hiring the Chappaqua School District's new superintendent. He made calls to offer his service and, he says, "People sort of chuckled and told me 'You'd have to have been here a little longer than you have in order to do that'." But those calls led to an invitation to serve on the committee that was drafting long-term goals; the people he called recognized that he knew something about organizations and about education.

The dialogue continued as he served on the committee, as well as at dinner parties and on the sidelines of the soccer fields of Chappaqua. Israelow was learning about his community, and the community was learning about him. He says, "I can't point back to a moment where I said 'I want to lead this school district to a commitment to continuous improvement.' It gradually emerged as I talked to more people about it." Israelow received a lot of encouragement to move from casual conversation to some kind of more concrete initiative.

"I was listening to the support I was getting," he says. "There was a level of interest from others that showed I was hitting the mark with something that was important to them." He was educating them, perhaps by bringing a community need to their awareness, or perhaps by simply providing an invitation to talk about something that had been bothering them. As the dialogue progressed, Israelow was also honing his message.

He also had to learn a few things about himself. "My own learning edge in terms of leadership is putting myself out there in more of an advocating, skillful, deliberate way," he says. Israelow's career in consulting had not prepared him for this task; consultants such as Israelow generally facilitate changes that others have decided upon rather than advocate for a particular kind of change. "It was the active part that I struggled with," he says. So as he was educating the community about the need for change, he was also learning about himself as a leader. He was learning to mobilize himself while beginning to mobilize others.

The salient points of Israelow's story are that messages were being exchanged between a leader and his followers, and those messages evoked learning—a new basis from which to think and act. Israelow and Chappaqua were thinking together. That thinking and learning continued as Israelow sought office, was rejected, then treated his second campaign with more deliberate attention to getting voters to the polls, and was elected.

As a leader relates his story, it raises questions, ideas, feelings, and other reactions in followers. A good story at least awakens the creative center of the mind. It may also roil the emotions, and rouse the spirit. Energy is created. The leader's primary task then becomes converting that energy into learning and committed action through this kind of extended and evocative dialogue. Such learning is a two-way street; leaders learn as well as followers.

Mobilizing in a Big Way

The processes that leaders employ in order to fulfill their responsibilities to enroll people, educate them, and help them to narrow the challenge will vary in complexity according to the size and nature of the group of people they lead. For example, in large organizations the leader's task often flies in the face of an entrenched culture that resists change, no matter how imperative the change might be. One such instance occurred in the late 1990s when Prudential Insurance (now Prudential Financial) prepared itself to meet the demands of a rapidly changing financial services business environment, and to convert from a mutual corporation owned by its policyholders into a publicly held company.

Jody Doele led and managed the program that was the centerpiece of Prudential's change effort. She later became vice president of Learning and Leadership Development for Prudential. Doele summarizes one of the central leadership problems the company faced: "Top-down communication wasn't working; the corporate culture at the time meant that information was a form of power, and it was hoarded." The effort that Prudential launched in 1997 to enroll all of its employees to commit to change involved 215 day-long meetings, each of them involving about 250 employees, and each of them led by two of the company's senior executives. The effort's objectives mirrored the three mobilization responsibilities of leaders: enroll all 50,000 employees in a change effort, educate them about the financial services industry and about Prudential's strategy to compete, and narrow the challenge so that each person can find ways to contribute. Educating all employees about the company's strategy was just the kind of information that had previously been, in Doele's terms, "hoarded."

The first task was to enroll Prudential's executives. A significant moment in that process occurred near the end of a meeting in which the executives were informed about plans to educate employees and about their roles in those plans. Doele asked the entire group of senior executives to serve as leaders for employee meetings and sign their names to a meeting calendar posted along a wall. Doele reports that the executives *swarmed* to the calendar. "They were three deep," she says, "Many came up to me and shared disappointment that they couldn't get a date!" Enrollment processes often benefit from ceremonies that encourage people to sign on formally. The second task was to educate employees, and Prudential developed a sophisticated set of learning materials to convey its story of change. And finally, processes and procedures were adopted to translate all of the energy generated by the effort into action by committed individuals.[5] Prudential's change effort can legitimately be viewed as 50,000 people thinking together about what they each must do to give life to their commitment to the organization.

An Attitude of Invitation

The fourth leadership responsibility for mobilizing followers is conveying trust, respect, and optimism during the course of enrolling people, educating them, and helping them to narrow the broader challenges. *Invitational theory* is the name used by a number of scholars and researchers to identify and examine the assumptions that will create an environment that helps people develop all facets of themselves. Such an environment fosters intellectual, emotional, and spiritual commitment because it encourages expression of mind, heart, and spirit.

William Purkey, a professor at the University of North Carolina Greensboro, defined invitational theory when he wrote, "Invitational theory is a collection of assumptions that . . . provide a means of intentionally summoning people to realize their boundless potential in all areas of worthwhile human endeavor."[6] Invitational theory holds that inviting others to realize their potential involves ongoing interaction. This and the previous chapter have shown the importance of such interaction as leaders tell their stories, engage in dialogue, educate, and mobilize. Purkey wrote a fine summary of these two chapters: "Leaders enlist others in their visions because they are capable of sharing their thoughts in vivid colors and compelling metaphors."[7]

Invitational theory provides a perspective about the assumptions that will enable leaders to effectively invite people during the course of their interactions with them, and regardless of the content of their insights and visions. There are four such assumptions and they are interconnected—respect, trust, optimism, and intentionality. Together they create the environment in which people are summoned to develop their full potential.

The first assumption, *trust,* means acknowledging that people will find their own best way of contributing when they are in an inviting environment. Leaders who hold this assumption are able to avoid micromanagement. They encourage individual initiative. They help people narrow challenges by educating them about what is needed in a broad sense, then leaving the specifics of implementation to them. They do not dictate what actions are needed.

The second assumption, *respect,* refers to the belief that people are able, valuable, and responsible. Leaders who hold this assumption find the right person for the right work and leave them to do what they can. The third assumption, *optimism,* rests upon the belief that people possess untapped potential (there will be more to say about optimism in Chapter 8).

Finally, the fourth assumption, *intentionality,* refers to the complex process of consistently and purposefully acting in a way that invites the development of the people being invited. In other words, *intentionality* means consistently and purposefully trusting and respecting people, and expressing optimism. Invitational theorists recognize that environments such as those created by leaders are dependent on the people in that environment, the physical setting, and the policies, programs, and processes that also contribute to the environment.[8]

Leaders may express the assumptions they hold about people either overtly or subtly, but their expression is unavoidable. When leaders who win high commitment are telling their stories, when they are in dialogue with followers, when they are educating and helping people narrow the challenge, they are, at the same time, doing so from assumptions of respect, trust, optimism, and intentionality. They are inviting people to participate in a quest and inviting them into an environment that fosters their own growth and allows their commitment to surface and flourish.

Development Strategies for Mobilizing

Even though Prudential's leadership effort involved more people than Israelow's, and presented more issues than Hollister's, the desired outcomes were the same: enrolled and educated people who have narrowed the overall challenge down to committed action. And the process—dialogue—was also essentially the same, involving all of the people whose commitment was needed. Whether it happens in one-on-one encounters, on the sidelines of a soccer field, or in a formal 250-person meeting at an airport hotel, leaders who want to mobilize others will have to help them decide upon the right things to do, set high expectations, let go of control, and work at setting an invitational climate.

Encouraging the Right Things

Sometimes leaders know precisely the right thing for followers to do in order to bring their visions to reality. Marvin Israelow, for example, knew that if fifty people would commit to enrolling twenty additional people, he would be elected and could promote continuous improvement in the Chappaqua schools. But, more often than not, leaders are so far removed from the work of their followers that they cannot know what should or might be done. When that is the case, leaders can still help followers discover the right things to do by preparing all of their intermediaries to engage with other followers in dialogue that will uncover and promote the right actions. In order to be effective, those intermediaries must be highly committed, articulate about the story of change that the leader wishes to tell, and prepared to help others answer three questions: *What can I do that I am not now doing? What do I now do that needs to be done better or more often?* and *What should I stop doing?*

Setting High Expectations

David Hollister was first elected mayor of Lansing by holding out a vision that the city, a middle-size, middle-America, middle-class community, and an underdeveloped capital city, should strive to become a world-class city. He said, "The thought of Lansing being a world-class city like New York or Toronto or London was just outrageous. I had a lot of people counsel me during the campaign to go for 'All-American'—something much more achievable. I felt offended by that." Hollister believed the asset base of the Lansing region had the components to become world-class. "So I decided to keep that mantra," he said, "and to carry it through everything I did."

During Hollister's nine years in office, the world-class terminology became woven into the fabric of Lansing. He said, "You see it on car advertisements and on other commercials. The teachers have picked it up, the local college uses it. It has become a standard." Lansing has not achieved the world-class designation, but Hollister achieved what he wanted—to mobilize the citizens of Lansing to work for a better city. "It set a very high bar," he said, "whether it was school reform, redeveloping downtown, a commitment to neighborhoods, better police protection, or negotiating with firefighters. I always used that criteria and made people think in stretch terms."

With pride and satisfaction Hollister told of a young boy who wrote a letter to the editor of a Lansing newspaper near the end of his tenure as mayor. The boy complained that his bicycle had struck a pothole and no world-class city would tolerate a pothole. Hollister said, "I was so elated by the fact that this had become such a criterion in a young person's mind. That he was using that measure to hold me accountable for his misfortune."

Letting Go

It is a popular axiom, and a correct one, but is far too often forgotten: "People support that which they help create." When attempting to mobilize people, leaders do best when they leave most decisions about implementing their insights and visions to those who are in the best position to make any particular decision. David Hollister left decisions about what it takes to be world-class teachers to the teachers, and left decisions about what it takes to be a world-class police force to the policemen.

A leader is not simply a super manager. Leaders tell their stories in clear and vivid terms so that mobilized followers will make the right decisions. Having done so, the leader's task is to let go of control, allowing people to create plans and actions that they will support and carry out.

Encouraging the Best in Others

William Purkey provides a metaphor for helping educators and students to become more aware of their involvement in creating an invitational environment. He calls it *the blue and orange card metaphor.* Blue cards are dealt to others each time the dealer is caring, respecting, or optimistic. Orange cards are dealt to others each time the dealer, in any way, informs another person that he is unable, worthless, and irresponsible. Orange cards cause pain. It is possible to give blue and orange cards to oneself as well as others. Every card counts—it has an impact. Purkey believes that it takes twelve blue cards to overcome the destructive impact of one orange card.

Leaders, like educators, ought to be aware of how many blue and orange cards they distribute, and how they do that. Blue cards encourage the best in people. Orange cards encourage escape; for leaders, escape means withdrawal of commitment. Purkey wrote, "It is increasingly clear that everything we do and every way we do it is orange or blue."[9]

Summary

When a leader is working from the base of a compelling insight, a noble vision, and a well-told story, she is positioned to mobilize the intellectual commitment that is created. In order to do so, the leader engages her followers in an extended dialogue that produces continuous learning—

for followers and for the leader as well. The leader also helps followers to ground the insight, vision, and story in their own activities; to decide how they can best contribute.

. . .

Questions About Yourself to Contemplate or Discuss with Others

Who, in your life experience, was practiced at mobilizing?

To what degree are you practiced at mobilizing?

What is it about mobilizing that rings true for your current leadership role?

How important is mobilizing to your further development as a leader?

Notes

1. Howard Gardner, *Leading Minds: An Anatomy of Leadership* (N.Y.: BasicBooks, 1995): 36.
2. Deepak Chopra in a speech to the Mobius Leadership Forum annual conference at the Harvard Business School, April 11–12, 2002. <http://www.mobiusforum.org/deepak.htm> (November, 2002).
3. David Bohm, *On Dialogue* (N.Y.: Routledge, 1996): 6–7.
4. William Isaacs, *Dialogue and the Art of Thinking Together: A Pioneering Approach to Communicating in Business and in Life* (N.Y: Currency, 1999): 2.
5. Tom Brown, "Communicating and Aligning via One Prudential Exchange," *Management General* (2000), <http://www.mgeneral.com/1-lines/00-lines/030004px.htm>.
6. William W. Purkey, "An Introduction to Invitational Theory," *International Alliance for Invitational Education* <http://www.invitationaleducation.net> (June, 2003).
7. William W. Purkey, "Blue Leader One: A Metaphor for Invitational Education," *International Alliance for Invitational Education*, <http://www.invitationaleducation.net> (June, 2003).
8. Purkey, "An Introduction to Invitational Theory."
9. Purkey, "Blue Leader One."

PART 2

WINNING EMOTIONAL COMMITMENT

LEADERS HAVE NO MORE IMPORTANT OR MORE POTENT TOOL than themselves. They are the primary expression of their stories. Their artistic mediums—mind, emotion, and spirit—are not separate from who they are as people. They are the medium and they are the message. As previous chapters have shown, their lives, insights, and vision all contribute to winning intellectual commitment. But their lives and their insights are in the past, and their vision is about the future. Winning emotional commitment is more a function of how a leader relates to others in the present than it is a function of the past or the future. This form of commitment flows from how leaders are seen to conduct themselves on a day-to-day and moment-to-moment basis, and particularly when those days and moments are laden with emotion. It is during such times that leaders must make speedy or spontaneous choices about how they will behave in relation to their circumstances and to others.

There are three leadership competencies involved in winning emotional commitment: *self-awareness, emotional engagement,* and *fostering hope.* Self-awareness is a precondition for emotional engagement. When such engagement occurs, a leader then has the opportunity to tap into constructive emotional energy and to transform unconstructive emotions. He can then also foster the hope that is a foundation for committed action. This process is shown in Figure Part 2-1.

SELF-AWARENESS  EMOTIONAL ENGAGEMENT FOSTERING HOPE

Figure Part 2-1. The process of winning emotional commitment.

Much can be achieved when followers are mobilized by a leader's insight, vision, and storytelling ability—when they become intellectually committed. When they also feel hopeful, emotional commitment can arise, and emotional commitment can work in tandem with intellectual commitment, becoming a far more powerful force than either is alone. The words of Jacob Bronowski, first cited in Chapter 1, are worth repeating here: ". . . the intellectual and the emotional commitment working together as one, has made the Ascent of Man."

6

Self-Awareness

I think your only salvation is in finding yourself,
and you will never find yourself unless you quit preconceiving
what you will be when you have found yourself.

—ROBERT HENRI

ust as a compelling insight forms the foundation of a leader's effectiveness at winning intellectual commitment, so self-awareness is the necessary foundation for winning emotional commitment. Self-awareness means tuning into one's own inner world. Daniel Goleman wrote that self-awareness is "the keystone of emotional intelligence."[1] Without self-awareness leaders cannot even recognize or acknowledge their own emotions, let alone manage them in anything approaching an able fashion. Without it, significant personal growth is unattainable, and empathy—a leader's ability to connect with the emotions of others—is impossible. When leaders are unable to connect with the emotions of others, winning emotional commitment is beyond their reach.

Gary Zukav, scientist, philosopher, and award-winning author of *The Seat of the Soul*, wrote, "Emotions are currents of energy that pass through us. Awareness of these currents is the first step in learning how our experiences come into being and why."[2] Emotions are reactions to both our environment and our thoughts. They then create further thoughts as well as behavior, thus participating vitally in an endless cycle of experience.

Bring on the Feeling

The previous four chapters have shown the competencies that leaders exhibit in order to win intellectual commitment: insight, vision, storytelling, and mobilizing. As the model of levels of commitment in Chapter 1 shows, intellectual commitment alone is limited. Intellectual commitment is based on understanding a leader's story, and understanding does not necessarily lead to action. Emotional commitment, on the other hand, impels people to act—to do something about the new understanding intellectual commitment produces.

Jim Wold made clear the need for leaders to seek emotional commitment when he said, "One of the mistakes that I have made in leading is that in having an intellectually great idea, you can lose connection with a group because you have thought it through so often. The emotional piece is really the glue, the connection, with the group."

If leaders are to have any hope of winning the kind of sustainable commitment that will create significant change, they must also pay attention to winning emotional commitment. Winning emotional commitment is not an entirely separate thing from winning intellectual commitment. It must be woven into the fabric of activities to win intellectual commitment so that emotional commitment is won during the course of telling a story and mobilizing people. We will treat it separately here only to highlight it as a crucial element of winning commitment from others, and to examine it more closely.

Experience in the Moment

Self-awareness is the foundation upon which any attempt to win emotional commitment must be constructed. Self-awareness is alertness to what we do, to how we feel, and to what we think. It is not psychoanalysis: It does not require examining the causes of thoughts and feelings, merely their recognition. It is not introspection, as that usually involves trying to solve a problem or understand something in a new way. When self-awareness is present, it is simply present, gliding along in the same way as behavior. It cannot be forced. It must, rather, be allowed to occur.

Just as we sometimes inhibit our behavior with judgment, or fear, or a variety of other obstructions, so we also inhibit self-awareness; many of the methods for developing it involve removing whatever barriers we have erected in order to keep ourselves unaware. Any thought that takes us away from the moment we are in obstructs self-awareness. And sometimes self-awareness means paying attention to thoughts and feelings that we would prefer to ignore.

Practitioners of Zen call this awareness of self in the moment *mindfulness*. Vietnamese Zen master Thich Nhat Hanh says, "You must know how to observe and recognize the presence of every feeling and thought which arises in you."[3] Self-awareness is not a separate activity and does not require sitting cross-legged in a quiet space. Thich Nhat Hanh spoke of "washing the dishes to wash the dishes," meaning that while washing the dishes he becomes completely aware of the act. He describes washing the dishes with awareness in this way:

> Wash the dishes relaxingly, as though each bowl is an object of contemplation. Consider each bowl as sacred . . . do not try to hurry to get the job over with. Consider washing the dishes the most important thing in life.[4]

The point of self-awareness is to attend to what is happening at the moment, to not allow the mind to be sucked into ruminations about the past or the future, and to not place ourselves at the whim of transitory emotion. When attention is focused on the moment in this way, it becomes possible to recognize the thoughts and feelings that arise within. Then, says Thich Nhat Hanh, "There is no way I can be tossed around mindlessly like a bottle slapped here and there on the waves."[5]

Self-awareness requires alertness to both thoughts and feeling because thoughts give rise to feelings and feelings give rise to thoughts. We will, however, focus here on feelings because the challenge for the majority of leaders in Western cultures is to reach beyond intellect when seeking commitment. Western culture prizes intellect above emotion. We like rationality, order, and logic. We are uncomfortable with that which cannot be thoroughly elucidated or quantified. Our schools emphasize training the mind over developing emotional intelligence. Prospective leaders whose gifts reside in the intellectual realm, and who wish to win emotional commitment, will have to extend themselves to learn the competencies needed to do so; their training does not ordinarily prepare them.

Tossed Around Mindlessly

When self-awareness is present it is nearly invisible to others, who normally see only its effects, and not its actual workings. The same is true when self-awareness takes a holiday. At such moments we look at the unmindful person in front of us and wonder, "What could he be thinking?" Here is an example of self-awareness on a holiday.

> *A senior executive of a large corporation was asked to lead a meeting of nearly 300 employees during which he would talk with them about the company's challenges and its plans to meet those challenges. He was comfortable talking about the hard bottom-line aspects of the message. But he was not so comfortable with his boss's expectation that he would also speak from the heart about*

the overall mood of the organization, and respond to comments and questions about employee morale. In other words, he was comfortable with the part of the story that needed to be told in order to win intellectual commitment, but not nearly so comfortable with what he had to do to win emotional commitment. He was, in his owns words, "a numbers guy."

He was also quite practiced at ignoring his own emotions and so, emotions being the persistent devils that they are, his discomfort grew into near-panic. Which he also ignored. He was quite accomplished as a public speaker when he had a prepared speech in his hands, and he believed that his experience would carry him through. But the success of the meeting required a generous measure of improvisation, which depends on self-awareness. It also required that he acknowledge and respond to the feelings that his message was sure to raise. Without awareness of his own feelings, this task was beyond his reach. What happened to him in the meeting is well described by Gary Zukav: "When we close the door to our feelings, we close the door to the vital currents that energize and activate our thoughts and actions."[6]

Just before the meeting began, he received information that the audience did not yet have. A corporate reorganization was in the works and important decisions had been made on the previous afternoon about which executives would be filling the high-level positions on a new organizational chart. This matter was not on the already fully packed meeting agenda.

When he took the speaker's platform to open the meeting, the unacknowledged stew of emotions that had been bubbling within him threatened to boil over. He did what he was used to doing; he retreated from the emotions. He told the audience that he had important news for them, picked up a marking pen, turned his back to the 300-person group, and began drawing the complex new organizational chart on a piece of paper on an easel. The drawing was too small for anyone to read other than those in the

*very front of the room. For an agonizingly long five minutes he
stood with his back turned while his audience wondered what he
was doing, why he was doing it, what people he was talking about,
and why it should matter to them. More than a few eyelids flut-
tered and nearly closed.*

There were, of course, many actions this man might have taken in order
to create a more positive outcome. But all of these actions depended on
self-awareness; the possibility of a different outcome was precluded by
his avoidance of uncomfortable emotions. He responded to his fear without being aware of it. In fairness to him, and to the many executives like
him, he had spent his entire career in an organization in which tight
scripts were the norm rather than improvisation. In this organization, a
good story was supposed to reside in numbers, charts, and graphs, and
such a story was thought to be all that was needed to inspire people. As a
result, political commitment and intellectual commitment were coin of
the realm. He had no meaningful experience to draw upon in a situation
where emotional commitment was required in order to produce significant and sustainable organizational change. This history, combined with
his preferences for intellect and for avoiding his emotions rather than
being mindful of them, worked together to undermine his attempt at
leadership, leaving him "tossed around mindlessly."

A Potter at Work

Unlike this executive, people with highly developed self-awareness are
able to experience both whatever is going on around them and whatever
is going on inside themselves, as well as the relationship between the two,
almost simultaneously. They may be tossed around, but it is not mindless.

M. C. Richards is a potter, poet, and author of the book *Centering*
(she and I are not related). I once sat beside her as she worked at her
potter's wheel. She was trimming a small cup. She spoke as she worked
in order, I suppose, to allow a glimpse into her creative process. She said

something like this, addressing the cup as it rested on the wheel: *I think you are too heavy at the bottom so I will shave a bit of clay and make you lighter and more balanced.* She removed a slice of clay from the cup's bottom. *Now . . . let's see what Dick thinks of you.* She handed the cup to me and I held it first in both hands, then in my right hand as I normally would hold a cup. "Feels good to me," I told her while wondering what qualified me as any kind of expert in the matter. She took it from me and weighed it in her own hands. *You still seem heavy to me, but Dick thinks you are all right. I wonder . . . are you really all right and am I the problem? Am I afraid that someone will judge me to be a poor potter if I let you go into the world this way? Will my fear cause me to make you lighter than you are supposed to be? Will my insecurity ruin you? Well, yes, I am afraid of being judged a poor potter, but I really do think you are too heavy at the bottom.* Then she removed the cup from the wheel and continued trimming.

In this small episode, Richards is aware of her surroundings—of her hands at the potter's wheel, of the cup, and of me sitting beside her. She is also aware of her own thoughts and feelings, and of how they might influence her work. She is aware of a desire to somehow include me in her process and make it more transparent to me, so she speaks her internal dialogue aloud and she hands me the cup. She has knowledge of her fear and insecurity, and wonders about the effect these emotions might have on her product. She does not want the cup to feel unbalanced and also does not want to ruin it because of self-doubt. Finally, she makes a judgment that her fear and insecurity are in fact getting in the way; they are causing her to mistrust what she can sense with her hands—the cup really is too heavy at the bottom. She is aware of all of these things almost simultaneously.

Those trained in the arts are, in general, more practiced in self-awareness than those who are not. Art is obviously a form of self-expression, so self-awareness is more obviously integral to the work. Leadership, as an art, is also self-expression, so leaders must be just as self-aware as any other artist.

The executive who got tossed around mindlessly did so because he was unwilling or unable to acknowledge the value and significance of his fear. When he pushed his fear aside rather than acknowledging it, he relinquished any possibility of mastering himself in an unfamiliar situation, and any possibility of artfulness as a leader. Richards is aware of her fear and its significance—its potential consequences to her work. She sees it lurking in the shadows of her self, and so it is far less a danger.

Richards is dedicated to drawing the analogy between her work at the potter's wheel and the work of forming a whole person. "It is not the pots we are forming, but ourselves," she wrote.[7] Because of her dedication to that purpose she integrates what she feels into her work process in a way that illuminates the work and allows her to make judgments about what she is doing based upon her sense of quality rather than upon her fears.

The Talk

Dawn Gutierrez also sometimes sees difficult feelings lurking in the shadows of her self. When she became executive director of New Way Learning Academy, she had to come to grips with the fact that not everybody on the staff she inherited was interested in hearing her ideas or her feedback. "I had some hurt feelings," she says. This is self-awareness—a simple acknowledgement of a feeling. When it is present, it seems obvious, unremarkable, and hardly worth mentioning. Yet its absence can be disastrous for a leader, as the executive in the story above discovered.

Because Gutierrez is aware of feeling hurt, she is able to do something productive about it. She says, "I came to the realization that not everyone would like me. That was hard because I am a people-pleaser." Gutierrez works at separating complaints about decisions she has made from complaints about her personally. She says, "I had to learn that it wasn't about me, or about me being right or wrong, it is about what I need to do to get the job done. It is hard. There are still times when it hurts a little bit, and I just give myself the 'It's not about me' talk." Her self-awareness provides her with the opportunity to adopt a different way of thinking about situations in which her ideas are met with resistance or rejection.

Like Richards, Gutierrez relies on being clear about her sense of purpose. When she is unclear about her purpose she harbors self-doubt, and then criticism from others seems to strike home because it contains a grain of truth. She advises, "If you stay focused, and you stay on what is right for the greater good then you are going to be all right with that criticism." This understanding is a direct product of self-awareness.

Noticing and Valuing

Richards and Gutierrez both overruled their feelings; Richards by deciding to make her cup lighter, and Gutierrez by giving herself "the talk." Overruling a feeling is one, but not the only choice a leader might make. Rabbi Zalman Schachter-Shalomi, for example, responded to feeling "anxious and out of sorts" about his age by taking the retreat that spawned his insight about the elder years. Bonnie Wright reacts to her regrets about not taking enough time for reflection by making sure that she now does take enough time. When they are acknowledged and accepted, emotions that do not need to be overruled can act as clues that something ought to change. Difficult feelings, in particular, are clues that something ought to change—that we either need to do something differently or to think differently.

All feelings obey the *paradoxical theory of change,* which states that *change occurs when one becomes what he is, not when he tries to become what he is not.*[8] When a leader experiences anger, frustration, hurt, loneliness, or any other feeling, it will not change until self-awareness arrives on the scene. It may be driven underground where it does its work in much the same way as a computer virus, wreaking havoc on the psyche and creating peculiar behavior, while remaining undetected. Awareness of the emotion provides a leader with a choice that would otherwise be made on the basis of whim or habit, a basis having nothing at all to do with the question at hand. Goleman says, "The goal is balance, not emotional suppression: every feeling has its value and significance."[9]

When leaders are practiced at self-awareness, they are then capable of responding to the emotions of others in ways that win emotional commitment. The paradoxical theory of change also applies when leaders must deal with the unconstructive feelings of others. Every leader would love to transform those unconstructive feelings into the enthusiasm that marks emotional commitment. Such a transformation becomes possible when leaders acknowledge those unconstructive feelings; when they allow others to be who they are rather than who they want them to become. There will be more to say about this in Chapter 7.

Development Strategies for Self-Awareness

Leaders can develop self-awareness, but it needs exercise. Meditation is certainly a proven way, whether it is the kind that requires sitting in stillness or the kind practiced by Thich Nhat Hanh, who speaks of being mindful during mundane activities such as washing the dishes or taking a walk. There are also some very simple ways to exercise self-awareness that can easily be integrated into a daily routine.

Finding the Barriers

Most of us who have been raised in a culture that values intellect and devalues feeling harbor rationalizations that create barriers to our own self-awareness. Those barriers are significant hurdles for leaders who wish to win emotional commitment. One of the first steps, then, in developing self-awareness is to become aware of the barriers. Ask this question: *What do I tell myself in order that I may remain unaware of my feelings?* Some people disparage their feelings, convincing themselves that they are unimportant. Others try to analyze their emotions rather than experience them, and in the process drive the emotion out with flights of mental activity. Some believe displays of emotion are inappropriate and embarrassing. Some see emotion as a sign of weakness.

These barriers are often very difficult to spot because they become habitual and so seem natural and right. A clue to the barriers keeping us apart from our own emotions can be found in our reactions to the emotions of others. Do we feel embarrassed, irritated, angry, disgusted by the feeling of others? Why?

Tuning In to the Body

Feelings are physical responses. Many of our ways of illustrating feelings are metaphors describing physical sensations: "butterflies in the stomach" for anticipation, a "lump in the throat" for pride or for a rising joy. Tightness in the shoulders or arms may signal anger or frustration. Tension around the mouth and eyes may signal an emerging hurt. Tuning in to feelings means allowing ourselves to notice and be attentive to these physical responses. Once aware of the physical sensation, ask the question, *What is the feeling that goes with this?*

Slowing Discussion Down

The mind ordinarily becomes fully engaged when we are in discussion, and if we are trying to "win" the discussion, or to prove something about ourselves to someone else, the mind can run rampant. We stop listening because the mind is busy forming a response while the other person is talking. When we do that, we also stop listening to whatever emotions are being called forth within us.

Slow discussion down by not forming a response while the other person is talking. Instead, either listen intently and do nothing else but listen, or listen while at the same time tuning into the body to sense emotions forming. Or, pause before responding to both form the response and tune in to the body.

Reviewing Experience

Disturbing experiences, the kind that nag at us as a kind of unfinished puzzle, often contain emotional content that has gone unacknowledged. Take the time to review those experiences, not puzzling over them so much as reliving them, as if playing a movie on the screen of the mind. Often, the emotions that were present during the experience will resurface and can then be brought into awareness. This practice will not change anything about the experience itself, as that is past. But self-awareness will have been exercised.

Shunning "I Feel That . . ."

A common mistake made by those who set out to become more aware of their emotions is confusing their thoughts with their feelings. Confusing thoughts with feelings is, of course, not conducive to winning emotional commitment.

We can catch ourselves making this mistake whenever we use the phrase, "I feel that . . . ," as in "I feel that you disagree with me," or "I feel that he is reliable." What is said after the phrase "I feel that . . ." is always a thought and not a feeling. The statement, "You disagree with me," is a thought. The statement, "He is reliable," is a thought. In order to get beyond the thought to the feeling ask, *What is the feeling that accompanies the thought?* How do I feel about the fact that I think you disagree with me? How do I feel about the thought that he is reliable?

Practicing an Art Form

Important facets of leadership are shared with all of the other art forms: Facets such as finding one's own voice, seeing things in different ways, navigating the turbulent waters of the creative process, meeting the challenges of self-expression, and submitting to the discipline of mastering a medium. Leaders who wish to master the leadership art will benefit greatly from serious study and practice of another art form as well. Bill Strickland made the point this way: "I think that a lot of the things that arts people talk about are qualities that have transferability into other areas of life."

Summary

A leader's ability to tune into his or her internal world—especially her emotional world—is a necessary foundation for engaging emotionally with followers and winning emotional commitment. A leader's awareness of feelings invites others to bring their own emotions forward as well. Self-awareness is a moment-to-moment process that prevents leaders from being subject to unacknowledged feelings and to the inept behavior that such feelings often produce.

• • •

Questions About Yourself to Contemplate or Discuss with Others

Who, in your life experience, was practiced at self-awareness?

To what degree are you practiced at self-awareness?

What is it about self-awareness that rings true for your current leadership role?

How important is self-awareness to your further development as a leader?

Notes

1. Daniel Goleman, *Emotional Intelligence* (N.Y.: Bantam Books, 1995): 43.
2. Gary Zukav, *The Seat of the Soul* (N.Y.: Fireside, 1990): 61.
3. Thich Nhat Hanh, *The Miracle of Mindfulness: A Manual on Meditation* (Boston: Beacon Press, 1976): 37.
4. Ibid, 85.
5. Ibid, 4.
6. Zukav, *The Seat of the Soul*, 60.

7. M. C. Richards, *Centering: In Pottery, Poetry, and the Person* (Middletown, Conn.: Wesleyan University Press, 1989): 13.
8. Arnold R. Beisser, "The Paradoxical Theory of Change," in Joen Fagan and Irma Lee Shepherd, eds., *Gestalt Therapy Now* (N.Y.: Harper & Row, 1971): 77–80.
9. Goleman, *Emotional Intelligence*, 56.

7

Emotional Engagement

Do not engage to find things as you think they are.

—HENRY DAVID THOREAU

Chapter 5 described the importance of a leader's ongoing dialogue with his followers as a vehicle for winning their intellectual commitment. Such dialogue is described as a "flow of meaning in the whole group." It is marked by the desire to create a new understanding within the group; an understanding that leads to action upon a common purpose. This dialogue is important to enrolling and educating followers and to helping them discover their own ways of contributing. Dialogue is described as *thinking together. Emotional engagement* between a leader and followers is the emotional equivalent of their intellectual dialogue with one another. Rather than describing the flow of meaning in a group, emotional engagement describes the *flow of feeling.*

Emotional engagement is *feeling together*. It is a critical competency for gaining emotional commitment.

Michael Jones provided a metaphor for conceptualizing the leader's role in both thinking together and feeling together with followers. When asked to describe what happens between himself and an audience listening to him play piano, Jones said, "There is a feeling of connectedness. In that moment I am speaking for the whole. I am capturing a truth that all of us resonate with. I am able to bring it into form. I am a medium for the current that is moving within the group and am able to capture and articulate that field of energy so it becomes available for all of us." Leaders who win emotional commitment begin to do so by acting as a medium for the emotional energy that is moving within the group, making that energy more available.

Inviting Emotion to Be Present

No leader can win emotional commitment unless emotion is permitted to be present; emotions, like ideas, need air time. Too often, however, would-be leaders discourage or suppress emotion in favor of intellect. They do so partly because they hold the unexamined belief that intellectual commitment is enough, partly out of personal preference, and partly because their training has honed their intellectual competency at the expense of their emotional competency.

Those who hold positions of leadership and who discourage or suppress emotion are usually least tolerant of emotions they judge to be unconstructive to their insights, visions, and attempts to mobilize others. Such emotions are often classified as "negative." But emotions themselves are neither positive nor negative. For example, anger might be considered positive if it is about something a competitor has done, but negative if it is about something a colleague has done. From a leadership standpoint, it is best to avoid classifying emotions as either positive or negative, but as more or less constructive to bringing a vision to reality. Leaders who discourage or suppress emotion fail to recognize that all emotion is energy, whether the emotion is or is not constructive to the leader's common purpose with followers. The leader's task regarding emotion is to help people transmute energy of any kind into emotionally committed action through emotional engagement.

There are four primary facets to a leader's emotional engagement with followers: first, the ability to manage her own emotions; second, the ability to make creative use of the self; third, the ability to empathize with followers; and fourth, proficiency at helping others to transform their uncomfortable or unconstructive emotions into committed action.

Self-Management

A few definitions will be useful when thinking about the first of the four facets of a leader's emotional engagement with followers—the ability to manage his own emotions. *Self-awareness*, as described in Chapter 6, is moment-to-moment alertness to what we do, how we feel, and what we think. *Self-knowledge* is recognition of the various aspects of the self that we carry around with us everywhere we go, such as our typical ways of reacting, the aspects of ourselves we prefer, and the aspects we would rather keep hidden. While self-awareness is alertness to the moment, self-knowledge is alertness to the totality of what we know about ourselves.

A third useful term is *self-management*. Daniel Goleman, Richard Boyatzis, and Annie McKee describe self-management as, among other things, managing disturbing emotions and impulses, being open with others about the self, and adapting to new challenges.[1] Self-management then is a decision-making process and, in particular, a practice of choosing behavior. It rests upon both self-awareness and self-knowledge; we cannot manage what we are not alert to. In relation to emotions, Goleman, Boyatzis, and McKee say that, "Self-management . . . is the component of emotional intelligence that frees us from being a prisoner of our feelings."[2] In other words, if we can recognize the presence of potentially destructive emotions, we can then choose to behave in ways that do not allow them to fulfill their destructive potential. For leaders this means choosing to behave in ways that maintain or win commitment.

When self-management is shut down we "give in" to our emotions, acting impulsively and usually ineffectively. Self-management is an attempt to avoid giving in to emotions, while at the same time recognizing and valuing their presence in a state of full self-awareness. The ultimate goal of any leader's self-management is to enable her to lead in a way that makes best use of who she is, is most personally fulfilling, and is best for the group of people or the organization from which commitment is being sought.

Creative Use of Self

The second facet of a leader's emotional engagement with followers is the ability to make creative use of the self. Leaders who win emotional commitment generally possess a varied repertoire of behavior and of sub-selves. David Hollister said, "You have multiple selves and you use different ones at different times." Hollister thinks of himself as a visionary. "I enjoy reading about the future," he said, "I like to study and think about what is going on around the world." He understands that sometimes this aspect of who he is needs to be front and center. There are other times when he is a strategist—a pragmatic and political realist, setting aside his vision temporarily.

Leaders have many options for choosing aspects of who they are that they might draw upon at any particular moment. They are multifaceted human beings and, unlike many other people, they give reign to their various facets and work to develop them, even those that at first seem unnatural. They strive to be thoughtful, empathetic, visionary, strategic, challenging, questioning, reverent, funny, withdrawn, outgoing, or any of many other qualities, all genuinely and all at the right moment. Leaders consciously choose who they will be—what aspect of themselves they will show—at any particular moment or in any particular circumstance.

Creative use of self is especially important to emotional engagement because leaders who can make conscious choices about who they will be at any particular moment are unlikely to be at the mercy of transitory feelings or impulses. They are also unlikely to mistake the present situation for one from the past and operate out of assumptions that do not hold. In making these choices, they must take care that the part of themselves which shows up is consistent with the story they are telling. If the story is serious they must not make light of it, if it is about compassion it cannot be told offhandedly, if it is about joy it must be told joyfully. Making these choices requires a leader to observe two places at the same time. The first place is the situation at hand; the second place is inside them.

Creative use of self is, then, a crucial element of a leader's storytelling ability. When creative use of self is happening in front of an audience, the people in the audience will have the response described earlier by Odds Bodkin, "They say, wow, this person is creating before my eyes." Improvising and storytelling are not just about the story; they are also about the identity of the leader. The leader's abilities to make creative use of self while improvising and storytelling help followers to answer the questions, *Who is this person? Is he trustworthy? Do I want commit to this insight, vision, mission, or cause? Can this person help me become better than I would otherwise be?*

An Absence of Empathy

The third facet of a leader's emotional engagement with followers is empathy. It is an elusive quality. When it is present, it is barely noticed. When we are with an empathetic person we think that she is likeable, understanding, a good listener, and perhaps sympathetic to our situation. But, like self-awareness, the absence of empathy can be very noticeable. Here is an example of a time and place where empathy was needed and it was absent. The story involves the executive team of a division of a multinational company. During the 1980s, the parent company had been having a rough time, punctuated by horrible press and by an across-the-board downsizing that was stunning because of the company's rock-solid reputation and long history of loyalty to its employees. The divisional executive team met to plan how to respond to the feelings of betrayal, fear, and resentment they knew were rampant among employees. At the urging of this team, the CEO of the parent company produced a video for them to use in employee meetings. The team wanted the CEO to issue reassuring words.

The divisional team began its planning meeting by comparing their perceptions of the state of employee morale with one another. Everyone agreed that the spirit of the company was at an all-time low. Then they watched the video for the first time. In it the CEO of their parent company sat stone-faced at his desk and spoke woodenly to the camera about how proud he was of the company and its employees, how he knew they were excited about the company's future, and how he "just knew" their usual pride and high morale were intact.

The man they saw in the video seemed so out of touch with the emotional state of his organization the divisional executives were at a complete loss about what to do. If they went ahead to develop plans to meet the current low spirit head-on, they would be in direct contradiction with the publicly expressed attitude of the CEO. If they did not go ahead, they too would seem out of touch; they would squander the opportunity to create an emotional bond with their employees and to transform unconstructive emotions into a renewed emotional commitment to the organization. They would also lose a chance to promote healing of the organization, and the morale problem would continue. They held the employee meetings without the video.

A leader who wishes to win emotional commitment—to win the hearts of followers—simply cannot do so in the kind of emotional vacuum created when feelings are ignored or denied. Emotions are ignored or denied when any feeling is considered unacceptable and when leaders, such as the executive in the story above, close their eyes to the pain in their organizations. Emotions are ignored or denied when organization members are encouraged to be "one big happy family" and never angry, lonely, or hurt. Emotions are ignored or denied when people misunderstand injunctions to "drive out fear" and instead fail to acknowledge fear where it exists, thereby encouraging others to be afraid of being afraid, and to be quiet about it. Emotions are ignored or denied when insincere celebrations are the norm, or when celebrating is the only sanctioned emotion. Emotions are ignored or denied when a group of people proceeds with the agenda that is on the table, while forgetting the vast sea of emotion sloshing just beneath the table, inevitably influencing whatever the agenda might be.

When emotions are ignored or denied, those in leadership roles miss the opportunity to lead because they are viewed as out of touch with their organizations, they do not get good information about the state of their organizations, they breed misunderstanding, and they fail to transform unconstructive emotional energy into emotional commitment. In doing so, they relinquish respect.

Empathetic leaders, on the other hand, are able to tune into the emotions of others, to value those emotions, and to accept them as legitimate even when they are uncomfortable or inconvenient to the leader's purposes. Empathy is at the core of what Goleman, Boyatzis, and McKee call *resonance*, being "in synch" with the mood of another individual or with the emotional tone of an entire group of people.[3]

Imagining Emotion

Empathy has two ingredients. The first is the experience of stepping into someone else's emotional world without getting lost in it. A useful metaphor is watching a movie in which we are able to enter the emotional world of the characters on the screen while remaining firmly in our own seats. We, the audience watching *Gone With the Wind*, know exactly how Scarlett O'Hara feels when she cries, "As God is my witness, as God is my witness, they're not going to lick me! I'm going to live through this, and when it's all over, I'll never be hungry again—no, nor any of my folks! If

I have to lie, steal, cheat, or kill! As God is my witness, I'll never be hungry again." We sense both her despair and her resolve.

We also know how Rhett Butler feels when he tells her, "Frankly, my dear, I don't give a damn." He is dismissing her, proud of doing so, and quite pleased for the opportunity to let her know about it. And we know how Terry Malloy, the washed-up fighter of *On the Waterfront*, feels when he says, "You don't understand! I could've had class. I could've been a contender. I could've been somebody, instead of a bum, which is what I am." We sense his keen disappointment about the course of his life.

Entering into the emotional world of another person requires a special kind of imagination—a *re-membering*, a putting back together, which involves returning to our own past feelings, or calling up feelings that are with us but that we do not readily acknowledge or express. This kind of imagination is not merely an intellectual "remembering" but also a return to the sensations that characterize the feeling: we may cry along with Scarlett, nod our heads in concurrence with Rhett, or squirm uncomfortably as our own sense of failure and loss resonates with that of Terry Molloy. When we re-member we reconnect with a part of ourselves.

As an audience, we are afforded the opportunity to step into the emotional worlds of Scarlett O'Hara, Rhett Butler, and Terry Malloy by virtue of watching their lives unfold on-screen. We enter their emotional worlds in our imaginations, sensitive to the changing flow of feeling in each of them and re-membering our own feelings. As we watch, we know it is not our emotional world, we know that our participation in it is temporary, and at the same time we know how they feel.

Of course, we can imagine how they feel only if we have developed the self-awareness that permits us such knowledge.

For some leaders it is easier to imagine the emotional worlds of their followers than it is for others. Alice Harris, known affectionately as Sweet Alice, is one such leader. At sixteen Harris was homeless, with two infant children and no food, and pleading for work in exchange for food and shelter. A woman offered her work, a small salary, and the use of a garage apartment. She asked in return that Harris help others in the future.

Today, some forty years later, Harris is executive director of Parents of Watts, an organization she founded. She oversees more than a dozen programs that provide emergency food and shelter, health seminars, legal and drug counseling, support for unwed mothers, and help to prepare young people for jobs and for college. The programs are housed in eight homes in Los Angeles that Harris owns. She has earned a degree from California State University and was honored in 2002 as the California lieutenant governor's Woman of the Year. She has been a panelist at Pepperdine University's annual Call to Leadership, and was inducted into the Hall of Fame of the Black American Political Association of California.[4] Her support is often courted by California politicians. One of her many fans said Harris may be the person most responsible for the relative peace of Watts since the riots of 1965.

When she talks about the people around her, Harris says, "I have worn the shoes of most of the people I have heard. I understand what they are going through. And I also understand that they have no resources. It is a pain that they have that people don't understand—a hard pain." Harris is able to imagine the pain of the people she helps because she too once felt that pain. "I have weathered that storm," she said.

This sense of wearing the shoes of the people they lead echoes from other leaders. Matt Catingub is the pops conductor of the Honolulu Symphony. He was named one of "10 Who Made a Difference" by the *Honolulu Star-Bulletin* in 2002 for his work in drawing top-notch talent to perform with the orchestra, for his musicianship, showmanship, and recordings, and for beginning the Music and Artists of Hawaii program to provide local musicians opportunities to perform with the symphony. Catingub can imagine the feelings of the musicians he selects for his bands because he has faced the same struggles they face. Wilma Mankiller can imagine the emotional worlds of other women, and of other Native Americans who have suffered prejudice, because she has suffered prejudice on both grounds. Rabbi Zalman Schachter-Shalomi can imagine the emotional worlds of anxious elders because he was also once anxious about growing old. Marvin Israelow can imagine the emotional worlds of other parents in Chappaqua who also want their schools to continuously improve.

It is clear that leaders have the best chance of winning emotional commitment from others when they are able to imagine the emotional worlds of their followers because they too have had the same or a very similar experience.

Communicating Understanding

The second ingredient of empathy is the ability to communicate to another person that his emotions have been understood and accepted. This communication requires a deep and honest caring about how other people feel, as well as avoiding attempts to minimize the importance of any feeling or to change it either by offering advice or judging it.

In the early stages of her career as an administrator and leader, a single incident taught Beverly O'Neill lessons about empathy that she says she will never forget. In 1994, O'Neill was elected mayor of Long Beach, California, the fifth largest city in the state and the thirty-third largest in the country. Four years later she was reelected, receiving nearly 80 percent of the vote. Long Beach prevents the name of an incumbent mayor from appearing on the ballot for a third term. However, in 2002, O'Neill was reelected as a write-in candidate. She was also elected as a trustee of the U.S. Conference of Mayors and president of the League of California Cities, and has received numerous awards for her work.

O'Neill recalls learning about empathy years before her electoral success, when she had responsibility for the buildings and grounds operations of a college. She had a corps of gardeners and another of custodians who worked for her. One custodian, a man in his fifties, came to her to tell her he was resigning.

"He was so upset, and so emotional," she said. "He was falling apart. The man started to cry. I was listening but I didn't know what the issue was. He was a good custodian, but here was this man in tears. He was quitting."

After much patient listening she began to understand. Gardeners were in charge of anything that was in the dirt; custodians of anything on the sidewalk. The tearful custodian had seen gardeners kicking cigarette butts out of the dirt and onto the sidewalk where they would not have to pick them up. O'Neill says that often, when she tells this story, people laugh. But it wasn't funny to her at the time.

"That taught me such a message about how relevant and irrelevant things are to different people," she said. "I couldn't believe he was so emotional about this issue. But when you visit it daily, and you are involved with it daily, you see it happen daily, and it affects you personally, you get to a breaking point."

She said, "I listened and I empathized with him. I told him, 'I can see how you are feeling about this because you are obviously so upset and so emotional about this issue. It is something that we can take care of.'" The custodian stayed at his job.

O'Neill's lessons? First, she said, "Issues are all relevant to the person that is talking about them." And beyond that, "You have to be prepared to listen. Sometimes that is all people want—to get something off their chest."

O'Neill also understands it is important for a leader to engage with emotions that are constructive to her common purpose with her electorate, and not just those that are unconstructive. She said, "It is important for me to be places where I can tell people what a great job they are doing and how important that is to the community. I love doing it. It isn't 'put on'— as if you have to thank people. I really mean to tell them—it is a heartfelt thing."

Practical Empathy

Many times people do want action from leaders as well as empathetic understanding. Leaders are not therapists. President Bill Clinton's catch-phrase, "I feel your pain," became a national joke in part because of his choice of words (he might have been better off saying "I can imagine your pain"), in part because people such as AIDS sufferers and Native Americans were not convinced that he could either feel or imagine their pain, and in part because many of the people whose pain he claimed to feel wanted more than that from him. Listening empathetically and communicating that one has heard and understood a person or a group of people can promote healing—people can become unstuck and can move past emotions that impede progress—but that is not enough. Healing alone will not give reality to a vision unless the vision is solely about healing.

Leaders also inevitably take actions that upset followers or those who they would like to have become followers. Beverly O'Neill, as a mayor who must balance the needs of different constituencies, said, "You have to say, 'If I were in your shoes I might feel the same way. But in my shoes I have to take into consideration this, this, and this.' I really understand how you are feeling, but I have to be responsible for more than just that." With this stance a leader acknowledges her differences of opinion with others, while also acknowledging the other person's feelings and offering the empathy that encourages emotional engagement and commitment.

Transforming Emotion

The fourth facet of a leader's emotional engagement with followers is his ability to transform the unconstructive emotions of followers into committed emotional energy. While unconstructive emotions may be difficult for leaders to hear, their expression is necessary. Leaders want emotional commitment; they want excitement about their visions and enthusiasm for their plans. When people experience excitement and enthusiasm, things get done. But emotions are interwoven with one another and are not easily isolated. Leaders cannot dismiss any unconstructive emotion without running the risk of also banishing the emotions that they want—excitement and enthusiasm.

Leaders who encourage the expression of unconstructive emotions grant themselves the opportunity to transform the energy of these emotions into more constructive emotions such as enthusiasm and hope. This transformation can occur when leaders allow unconstructive emotions to simply be what they are, and when they acknowledge them—when they communicate that the feelings have been heard and accepted. Remember that feelings obey the *paradoxical theory of change*—change occurs when one becomes what he is, not when he tries to become what he is not.[5] Feelings can change when they become what they are.

When unconstructive feelings are blocked from becoming what they are, they tend to get stuck. Then the person with the feeling is stuck—trapped in the emotion. When a person or group of people is stuck in an unconstructive emotion they are blocked from moving forward toward hope and positive action. It is as if the unconstructive emotion is caught in the throat, preventing the swallow of hope that would allow change to occur.

Beverly O'Neill sometimes faces the unconstructive emotions of constituents. Her natural inclination is toward people, and when she first began to take on leadership roles, she found it difficult to focus on the issues that came before her. "I felt like a square peg in a round hole," she said, "I was more interested in the person than the issue." Then she discovered that her ability to heed the emotional tone of others gave her an important advantage. She said, "If someone came to me very angry about an issue, by the time we talked about it, and they could see that I was interested in them, then the issue became . . ." and here she searches for just the right word to describe the transformation that takes place in such conversations, and concludes that it is, ". . . softer." In that statement, O'Neill describes what can happen when an unconstructive emotion is heard and valued by a leader—when the leader can empathize. The unconstructive emotion is transformed.

Development Strategies for Emotional Engagement

Self-awareness, the subject of Chapter 6, is a precondition for developing emotional engagement. Those who remain unaware of their own emotions have little or no hope of resonating with the emotions of others. But as self-awareness develops, so does the capacity for emotional engagement. Most people can be powerful sources and sensitive receivers of emotion, and when a leader and her followers can get on the same emotional page, emotional commitment becomes possible.

Practicing Empathy

Empathy is often presented as a simple set of skills such as listening and paraphrasing what we have heard. But the person who is most often quoted about empathy, psychologist Carl Rogers, saw it as much more than that. For Rogers, empathy is, "a complex, demanding, and strong—yet also a subtle and gentle—way of being."[6] Developing in this way of being begins with extending awareness by practicing a special kind of listening wherein a leader both grasps the other person's meaning and senses the underlying feelings at the same time. When a leader can do both—understand both the content and the emotions—he can then focus on imagining being in the shoes of the other person.

Focusing on Similarities

Emotional engagement between a leader and her followers can begin when the leader focuses attention on the similarities between them rather than on their differences. What hopes and dreams do we share? What feelings? The more a leader can see these similarities and concentrate on them, the greater the possibility of developing emotional engagement and winning emotional commitment.

Speaking the Unspeakables

Jim Wold likes to give people permission to *speak the unspeakables* during meetings. He explained, "The unspeakables are those things that are bothering you and you just don't know if you should say it or not." Speaking the unspeakables offers the opportunity for people to not only say what is on their minds, but also to diminish the anxiety and fear that is often a barrier to emotional engagement and emotional commitment. Of course, any leader who offers permission to speak the unspeakables needs to be willing to hear, acknowledge, and value whatever comes up.

Hanging Out

Beverly O'Neill points out that emotional engagement between a leader and followers is part of an ongoing relationship in which there is a free flow of information. "Communication never ends," she said, "You don't wait until you have an issue. You don't wait until you have a crisis. You don't wait until you just happen to call a meeting. Communication is constant. Communication is proactive." The purpose of the communication is not so much dissemination of information as it is building and maintaining the relationship that fosters emotional engagement and emotional commitment: "That is what you constantly have to work on."

Matt Catingub echoed O'Neill when he spoke of "hanging out" with his musicians to talk about life in general. And many of Marvin Israelow's conversations about improving Chappaqua schools occurred on the sidelines of the soccer fields where his son Jacob was playing. O'Neill said, "If you don't talk about the time of day—which is what most conversations are—about the weather, the children, the last holiday; unless you can talk on a human level you don't ever really communicate," And Bill Strickland put it very succinctly when he said of being a leader, "You have to stay in touch with human beings."

It is, of course, not always possible for a leader to "hang out" with every follower. Still, leaders can set a tone within their organizations that encourages a free flow of information that includes how people feel and what is happening in their lives. O'Neill said, "The CEO of a big company can be very concerned about the people he works with, and I hope that the people he works with are communicating the same concerns about the people they work with." As Monsignor Dale Fushek learned on the day he chauffeured Mother Teresa around Phoenix, "People don't give to things, they give to people." And, according to Beverly O'Neill, people will give to a leader who is continually, "Touching their life in some way."

Summary

A leader's emotional engagement with followers stands at the center of his attempts to win emotional commitment. The first leadership competency for winning emotional commitment—self-awareness—is a prerequisite for emotional engagement. The third—fostering hope—is a leader's *raison d'être* for emotional engagement.

Leaders who engage emotionally with followers are able to make creative use of the self, thereby avoiding placing themselves at the mercy of fleeting feelings. Just as important, they are able to empathize, imagining the feelings of others and communicating that these feelings have been heard and accepted as valid. When feelings have been heard and accepted, a leader then has the opportunity to capitalize upon the energy of constructive feelings and transform the energy of unconstructive feelings.

• • •

Questions About Yourself to Contemplate or Discuss with Others

Who, in your life experience, was practiced at emotional engagement?

To what degree are you practiced at emotional engagement?

What is it about emotional engagement that rings true for your current leadership role?

How important is emotional engagement to your further development as a leader?

Notes

1. Daniel Goleman, et al., *Primal Leadership* (Boston: Harvard Business School Press, 2002): 254.
2. Ibid, 46.
3. Ibid, 5.
4. Eric Rapp, "Charity, Service a Family Tradition for South Bay Division Operator Louvenia Harris," MTA News, <http://www.mta.net/press/stakeholders/scoop_stories/110_harris.htm>. Also "Sweet Alice Harris: A Biography," <http://www.calstat.org/sweet_alice.pdf> (January, 2003).
5. Arnold R. Beisser, "The Paradoxical Theory of Change," in Joen Fagan and Irma Lee Shepherd, eds., *Gestalt Therapy Now* (N.Y.: Harper & Row, 1971): 77.
6. Carl Rogers, *A Way of Being* (Boston: Houghton Mifflin, 1980): 142–143.

8

Fostering Hope

"Hope" is the thing with feathers that perches in the soul.

—EMILY DICKINSON

The emotion that is most significant to winning emotional commitment is hope, the feeling that something desirable is possible or is likely to happen. Hope has many faces and so attracts many descriptions. It has been called a weapon against intractable problems, a valuable possession, and a catalyst for change. Aristotle captured the fanciful face of hope when he described it as "a waking dream." Author Madeleine Blais, writing about an Amherst Lady Hurricanes high school basketball team determined to make it to the state championship and overcome a history of choking, concluded that, "Hope is a muscle."[1] Blais's characterization of hope suggests that it benefits from exercise and the right nutrition. Internet journalist Dorothy Anne Seese pointed to the catalytic face of hope when she called it, "The engine that drives all things." Samuel Johnson wrote that, "Hope is itself a species of happiness, and, perhaps, the chief happiness which this world affords."

Norman Cousins, almost totally paralyzed by a degenerative disease and given just a few months to live, eventually returned to work after treating himself with high doses of vitamin C and laughter. Cousins deemed hope to be independent of logic, and wrote, "The capacity for hope is the most significant fact of life." Pliny believed that, "Hope is the pillar that holds up the world." Best-selling author Anne Lamott described the challenging process of hoping when she wrote, "Hope begins in the dark, the stubborn hope that if you just show up and try to do the right thing, the dawn will come. You wait and watch and work: you don't give up." Vaclav Havel, who won several prestigious international literary prizes in addition to serving as president of the Czech Republic said, "Hope is a state of mind, not of the world." Educator, Yale University chaplain, and civil rights activist William Sloane Coffin, Jr. wrote, "Hope arouses, as nothing else can arouse, a passion for the possible."[2] Beverly O'Neill believes that, "Hope is the best thing you could provide anyone." One of the greatest sources of satisfaction in her role as mayor of Long Beach is "Every day you can provide hope for the future."

Leaders foster hope in four ways:

1. With their optimism about grounding their insights and visions in reality, and about the capabilities of others
2. With practical actions and successes
3. With the hopeful tenor of their personal stories
4. With the power of their insights and the nobility of their visions

Optimism, Pessimism, and Hope

The beginning, the initial spark that produces hope and builds emotional commitment is a leader's optimism. Optimism is a choice. The opposite choice, the alternative to optimism, is pessimism, which does have its own value. Pessimism is the tendency to view life's circumstances as troublesome, ominous, or futile. In an unsure and perilous world, pessimism helps us stay attuned to reality. Laurence J. Peter, of *Peter Principle* fame, wrote that, "A pessimist is a man who looks both ways when he crosses the street," which is a wise thing to do. Pessimism, however, is no basis for leadership. Winston Churchill said, "A pessimist sees the difficulty in every opportunity; an optimist sees the opportunity in every difficulty." Leadership is about seeing opportunities, not difficulties. Helen Keller, whose words more fully address the essence of leadership, wrote, "No pessimist ever discovered the secret of the stars, or sailed to an uncharted land, or opened a new doorway for the human spirit."

Martin Seligman has been studying optimists for more than thirty-five years. He wrote that the difference between pessimists and optimists is in how they habitually think about bad events or situations. Pessimists tend to believe that bad events have pervasive and permanent consequences and will undermine all of their efforts, rendering them helpless. Optimists, on the other hand, see any particular bad event or situation as limited to that one circumstance and as temporary.[3] In so doing, optimists restrict their feelings of helplessness.

Optimism and pessimism are each habits of the mind, and while pessimism has some utility, optimism is the healthier and more satisfying habit. The research of Seligman and others shows that optimism can ward off depression, can be a source of higher achievement, can enhance physical well-being, and is a more pleasing state to live in. Seligman concludes, "There can be little doubt about it. Optimism is good for us."[4] And, more to the point of leadership and winning emotional commitment, he wrote, "Finding temporary and specific causes for misfortune is the art of hope."[5]

The Art of Hope

Pat Croce is a leader who has mastered the art of hope. *Inc. Magazine* dubbed Croce "The Dale Carnegie of the 21st Century." "I think that is a supreme compliment," Croce said. He is most widely known for his work as president and part-owner of the Philadelphia 76ers. Croce engineered one of the most dramatic turnarounds in sports history, reshaping the 76ers, earning a berth in the 1999 National Basketball Association playoffs for the first time in eight years, and reaching the playoff finals in 2001. Along the way, attendance increased by 46 percent. During that time, Tom Friend, senior writer for *ESPN The Magazine* wrote of Croce, "There is no better sports CEO out there"[6] He is also recognized as the founder of Sports Physical Therapists Inc, which had forty sports medicine centers in eleven states before merging with Novacare, and as the author of several books, including the *New York Times* best-seller, *I Feel Great and You Will Too.*

Croce knows about life's disappointments and adverse events, and offered two examples. In 1977, when Croce graduated from physical therapy school, he wanted to become the physical therapist for the Philadelphia Eagles football team. "They slammed the door in my face," he recalled. Many years later, in his first year with the 76ers, when they were still losing, he had to fire both the general manager and the coach; difficult tasks for a self-described "people person." Today Croce says of these two experiences, "I think God gives us challenges so we become stronger. We have challenges that come our way, and at the time we can't understand why, but it just makes us stronger when we pursue our goals and visions." This is an optimist speaking. His defeats and difficulties are limited to specific circumstances and are temporary. Croce takes optimism even a step further than seeing setbacks as temporary and limited; he sees value in his defeats and difficulties, believing that they make him stronger.

A 1999 motorcycle accident tested Croce's optimism. His left leg was shattered when another cyclist skidded into him on wet pavement shortly after the beginning of a coast-to-coast motorcycle trip. The result was multiple surgeries involving bone and muscle grafts to save his leg. Croce's doctor told Tom Friend, "Through this whole thing, he had about ten minutes of post-traumatic depression, and people usually have that problem for months. He had about ten minutes."[7] Croce said that during his time in the hospital he asked himself, "Why you, Pat, why you?" His answer was, "Why not?"

Today, in true optimist fashion, he said, "I looked around on that hospital floor and saw kidney transplants and all kinds of really severe illnesses. Yeah, they had to graft part of my shoulder into my leg but that was nothing. Whenever I want to be grounded all I have to do is take a walk through McKee Rehabilitation Center and see all these patients who are paralyzed from the waist down or from the neck down, or bodies dysfunctional from stroke, that puts everything into perspective."

Success Is Always Possible

Wilma Mankiller knows that growing up in the Cherokee culture, with its emphasis on keeping the mind free of negativity, is the source of her optimism. One of her favorite Cherokee traditional prayers begins, "First let us remove all negative things from our mind so we can come together as one." She said, "The idea is that if we harbor negative thoughts—envy, greed, hate—those thoughts will soon permeate our being and prevent us from acting in a responsible way. Negative thoughts become negative actions." This Cherokee view is in harmony with modern thought and science: Martin Seligman wrote, "Our thoughts are not merely reactions to events; they change what ensues."[8]

"All my life," Mankiller said, "I have seen people in terrible circumstances who have managed to find something positive to focus on. They find some positive characteristic about even the most ardent opponent. They look back on trauma and pain and think about what lessons they learned. I have seen any number of people who live with almost no amenities but they know genuine love, deep friendship, and appreciate simple things like a good song or a lovely flower."

Like Croce, Mankiller's optimism was tested by physical challenges; she has had multiple surgeries to deal with a variety of afflictions. Still, her optimism does not wane. She said, "All my adult life, I have constantly tried to live in a positive way, free of as much negativity as possible." This optimism is necessary to her leadership because, she said, "Building clinics, working on federal legislation, or any other project requires knowledge of the subject matter and skill as well as absolute certainty that success is possible."

Pessimism has no value to leadership for Mankiller. She said, "Who wants to follow a leader who sits around wringing their hands and reciting a litany of problems?" Martin Seligman agrees. In *Learned Optimism*, he states flatly that, "Americans want optimists to lead them."[9]

Not Pollyanna

Croce's and Mankiller's optimistic outlooks do not avoid the problems of the moment. They have a kind of optimistic realism, an attitude that communicates to others that vision must be pursued even in the face of difficulties, and that commitment means, "the dawn will come. You wait and watch and work: You don't give up." Croce said, "I am not pie-in-the-sky, don't get me wrong. But my glasses are tinted rose-colored. I am not Pollyanna. I know there is negativity in the world. I know there is pessimism. I know we have losses. It's OK. I believe there is a reason for all of that, I just am not smart enough to understand the reason, so let's keep pursuing."

Beverly O'Neill echoed Croce's words when she explained her attitude about moving forward despite the kind of budget constraints that frequently plague cities: "We have a great future and we are going to be working toward that future even though our finances right now are in very bad shape." O'Neill said that, along with pursuing her vision of a better Long Beach, "You can't ignore the problems of the present."

Two Varieties of Optimism

The optimism of leaders such as O'Neill, Croce, Mankiller, and Harris appears in two ways. First, and most obviously, it shows up in relation to the insights and visions they and their followers are pursuing together. The second and less obvious way it appears is in relation to others: Leaders who win high levels of commitment are also optimistic about the capabilities of other people. Pat Croce said it very simply: "I am a big believer in people."

O'Neill asked the people in her office to identify something they might add to their job, something that would be fun for them. One man gave up his Saturdays to coordinate cleaning up the city with groups that wanted to work on that. A woman who has a special fondness for children developed a curriculum to take to schools. O'Neill said, "I really believe in the ability of people. Some of them have great qualities that have never been brought out." Bill Strickland, speaking of the students who attend Manchester Craftsmen's Guild and Bidwell Training Center, said, "There is nothing wrong with the kids that come here, except that they don't have an opportunity to show they are world-class citizens. You treat them that way and they will." And Alice Harris explained her rationale for being optimistic about the capabilities of others by saying, "God took a chance on all of us. You can't help people and not grow yourself."

William Purkey, articulating invitational theory, wrote that the assumption such leaders make is, "People possess untapped potential in all areas of human endeavor."[10] This assumption is grounded in the understanding that no clear limits to human potential have yet been discovered.

Successes and Personal Stories

A leader's optimism is not the only means to sustain hope and emotional commitment over the long course of effecting significant change. Practical actions and successes, and the hopeful tenor of a leader's personal story, can also provide hope, not only that *things can change*, but also hope that *we can change things*. The hopes of the people around Bill Strickland were certainly raised when Manchester Craftsmen's Guild won a grant from the National Endowment for the Arts. This grant became the catalyst for a $7.5 million capital campaign to construct a 62,000-

square-foot vocational training and arts center. The hopes of the Cherokee Nation were raised by Wilma Mankiller's success at helping the tribe
win a self-determination agreement, allowing it to assume responsibility
for Bureau of Indian Affairs funds. Matter-of-fact and on-the-ground
triumphs such as these are a source of pride and give impetus to further
hopes. If leaders and their organizations do not deliver such practical
achievements, their stories and mobilization efforts flounder. Their credibility wanes, frustration and cynicism mount, and then despair can drive
out hope.

Mary Ellen Hennen provided a story about how practical success can
fuel hope. Hennen launched the Minnesota State lottery as its director of
administration, and also serves on several not-for-profit boards. One of
her leadership roles, she said, is to, "Get people moving towards doing
things that they never thought they could do." In a former job, as executive director of the Public Utilities Commission of Minnesota, she inherited a small and inadequately equipped organization. She said, "They saw
themselves as a tiny poor agency having to make huge organizations toe
the line and do the right thing. They felt helpless. It drove me insane
because they were well educated and well positioned to do what they
wanted to do, but they were waiting for someone to tell them what to
do." In other words, there was no sense that *things can change*, let alone
any sense that *we can change things*. Jim Wold seconded Hennen's sense
that getting people moving fosters hope. He said, "People get hamstrung
by believing someone else is responsible. The line we really need to use is,
'What can we do right here and right now to make something happen?'"

Hennen discovered that her organization had no system to keep
track of all of the information it used to prepare public utility commis-
sioners to make decisions about utility rates. She saw an opportunity to
fuel the hope of the organization that it really could effect change. She
gathered a group of people to decide what kind of system would meet the
need. She also provided them with resources when asked. "I didn't know
what they needed," she said. "And I wasn't about to prescribe what they
needed. But I had to get them the resources." The first resource they

needed, she said, was, "That I trusted them. That had evidently never been done before." Then she got out of their way.

Hennen's group designed and won approval for a new integrated information system. She summed up the importance of such successes for building and maintaining hope when she said, "If you are not accomplishing something and you can't see something practical, your enthusiasm and your interest are not going to be captured for very long." The value of this experience to her organization went far beyond a new information system. The more important value was the sense that, in her words, "We can make a difference." That sense generates hope and emotional commitment.

Leaders also foster hope when their stories speak about how they overcame obstacles, or transformed themselves, or delivered a success. Wilma Mankiller's story of overcoming prejudice against women to become the first female chief of the Cherokee Nation can be a source of hope to other Cherokee women, as well as to other women who suffer prejudice. Alice Harris's transformation from an out-of-work teenage mother to the Sweet Alice Harris that is known throughout California, as well as in the corridors of the U.S. Senate, can be a source of hope to impoverished people anywhere. Bill Strickland's tale of growing up in a crumbling urban environment, committing himself to the potter's art, then becoming a much sought after expert on the relationship between the arts, business, and social responsibility can be a source of hope to anyone in any crumbling neighborhood.

Public Good or Private Goods

Along with their optimism, practical successes, and their own personal stories, a leader is also a source of hope when his vision has a noble quality to it. As described in detail in Chapter 3, such visions offer followers the opportunity to commit to something larger than their own self-interest. Such opportunities seem to occur less frequently than they once did. During the final quarter of the twentieth century Americans underwent a change in their thinking about what is important. Martin Seligman described the change as a shift from "the public good to private goods."[11] The combined weight of the assassinations of great social leaders, the Vietnam War, presidents and other leaders who disappointed and betrayed us, along with the failure of families and religious institutions to address the despair created by these distressing events, has left us with a famine of hope. As a result, we have turned our backs on noble visions in favor of a personal and self-centered satisfaction that is unfulfilling. We have a drive to work for the common good, and we are frustrating that drive. As Bonnie Wright said, "People need to help other people."

This shift in emphasis from the public good to private goods is mirrored in the visions of those in leadership positions when these visions are mostly about needs for personal achievement or about the prestige and accomplishments of their organizations, rather than about contributions to the common good. Such visions accept the shift from public good to personal satisfaction rather than challenging people to rise above their own interests, or to create a more equal balance between their own interests and the common good. Those in positions of leadership who capitulate to the shift from public good to private goods do not provide an adequate basis for hope, except for hope that is entirely self-centered and ultimately unfulfilling. Seligman wrote, "The life committed to nothing larger than itself is a meager life indeed.[12]

Developmental Strategies for Fostering Hope

The strategies listed below are of two kinds: strategies to foster hope in others, and strategies to help leaders develop and maintain their own optimism. Optimism is a habit, and is thus the achievable province of anyone. There are attitudes and strategies that anyone can adopt to help them develop the habit of optimism.

Celebrating Success

It has been said many times before and in many places, and it is worth repeating: Leaders must encourage the celebration of successes. Such celebrations validate the hope of the past and fuel the hope for the future. Celebrations do not have to be grand. For example, Jim Wold likes to begin every meeting with the people who work for him with the question, "What is going well?"

Doing the Impossible

What "impossible" thing could be accomplished by the people you lead that, having accomplished it, would fuel hope?

Assuming Self-Responsibility

One attitude in particular is essential to develop the habit of optimism. This attitude is one of seeing the self as the source of the self. It is sometimes referred to as *self-responsibility*. Those who are self-responsible acknowledge that they create their own thoughts and feelings. This is the opposite of victimization, in which people conclude that their thoughts and feelings are caused by some source outside of the self. The self-responsible person would be more likely to ask, "I wonder what it is about me that causes me to get angry at him," rather than to think, "He makes me angry." Leaders rarely, if ever, succumb to feeling victimized. They rarely abdicate their own responsibility for what they think or how they feel. Pat Croce said, "I should let you know, in reality, there are threads of negativity that enter into my gray matter, and then I have to fight them off." Croce knows that he is the source of his thoughts and feelings and that he alone can change them.

Listening to Self-Talk

Each of us has a running dialogue with ourselves. Developing a habit of optimism involves interrupting that dialogue when it becomes negative. Pat Croce hears the threads of negativity that cross his mind. Wilma Mankiller's beloved Cherokee prayer—*first let us remove all negative things from our mind*—assumes that one hears those negative things. Tuning in to the dialogue we are having with ourselves allows us to interrupt it when it becomes negative, and can help us spot the habits we have formed. Sometimes a simple, "Shut up!" to ourselves is very useful.

Hanging Out with Optimists

Bad stuff happens, and sometimes the people around a leader are draped in gloom, helplessness, and foul temper. Pat Croce said, "Regardless of how I wake up in the morning with a positive attitude there are nasty people and negative situations that arrive." Croce is very firm about this point: "Don't treat me with any whining, because I don't want to hear it," he said, "You want to whine about something, let me bring you to see Sister Mary and let's look at what she is doing with the homeless." Sister Mary is Mary Scullion, who the *Philadelphia Inquirer* called, "The tough-minded guardian angel of Philadelphia's homeless."[13] Mary Ellen Hennen said, "If you don't want to try, I will have a lot of problems with that." Alice Harris is equally as vociferous as Croce and Hennen are about people with negative attitudes. She said, "I don't like to deal with people around me with a 'can't' attitude. God didn't make us with a 'can't' attitude. We are made with power."

Any leader who wants to maintain the optimistic attitude that fuels hope will find pessimists draining. Warding off the negativity of others can soak up a lot of energy. Leaders who want to maintain their own optimism, and thereby have a better chance of fostering hope and winning emotional commitment, need a contingent of optimistic people around them. Not people whose optimism is of the Pollyanna kind, but people whose optimism has the same realistic element the leader's does.

Getting a Good Night's Sleep

Pat Croce has several strategies for maintaining his optimism. "One of them is sleep," he said, "I can guarantee you I am way more positive in the morning than at night." Wilma Mankiller concurs. She said, "Whenever I am feeling burned out or pessimistic, I simply get a good night's sleep."

Summary

Fostering hope is the third competency for winning emotional commitment, the other two—*self-awareness* and *emotional engagement*—being preconditions. The emotional commitment of others thrives best in an atmosphere in which the leader's self-awareness permits her to be emotionally engaged with followers, in which the validity of both constructive and unconstructive feelings is acknowledged, in which unconstructive feelings are transformed, and in which hope prospers. Leaders most often fail in their attempts to foster hope and win emotional commitment because they have not developed in themselves the underpinnings that create such an atmosphere. They are not self-aware, and so cannot resonate with the emotions of those around them, and can become caught in unproductive and inappropriate behavior. They are not emotionally engaged with their followers, and so do not have the opportunity to capitalize on productive emotions and transform those that are unproductive.

When a leader's self-awareness and emotional engagement are impoverished, his attempts to foster hope devolve into gratuitous cheerleading, stoic appeals to pride or personal achievement, and overreliance on rewards for performance. It is unavoidable that a leader will set the emotional tone for whatever group of people he leads. When a leader has developed the underpinnings—self-awareness and emotional engagement—and when he also assumes attitudes of respect and trust toward others, then the leader's optimism can be contagious; it can foster hope and can win emotional commitment.

• • •

Questions About Yourself to Contemplate or Discuss with Others

Who, in your life experience, was practiced at fostering hope?

To what degree are you practiced at fostering hope?

What is it about fostering hope that rings true for your current leadership role?

How important is fostering hope to your further development as a leader?

Notes

1. Madeleine Blais, *In These Girls, Hope Is a Muscle* (N.Y.: Warner Books, New York, 1995).
2. The sources of quotes in this chapter, unless otherwise noted and excluding those by leaders interviewed for this book, can be found at <http://www.brainyquote.com>.
3. Martin E.P. Seligman, *Learned Optimism*, (N.Y.: Knopf, 1990): 4–5.
4. Ibid., 291.
5. Ibid., 48.
6. Tom Friend, "Eyes on the Prize," *ESPN The Magazine*, <http://espn.go.com/magazine/friend_20010523.html> (April, 2003).
7. Ibid.
8. Seligman, *Learned Optimism*, 7.
9. Ibid., 207.
10. William W Purkey, "An Introduction to Invitational Theory," at *International Alliance for Invitational Education*, <http://www.invitationaleducation.net> (June, 2003).
11. Seligman, *Learned Optimism*, 284.
12. Ibid., 284.
13. "Sister Mary Scullion: The Tough-Minded Guardian Angel of Philadelphia's Homeless," *Philadelphia Inquirer* (December 25, 2000) (unsigned editorial).

~

PART 3

WINNING SPIRITUAL COMMITMENT

THE NEXT THREE CHAPTERS DESCRIBE THE COMPETENCIES FOR winning spiritual commitment: *rendering significance, enacting beliefs,* and *centering.* The character of the effort needed to win spiritual commitment is different from that of winning either intellectual or emotional commitment. Winning intellectual commitment and winning emotional commitment can each be described as processes with preconditions and outcomes. Insight and vision are preconditions for telling a compelling story, which in turn produces the opportunity to mobilize people and win intellectual commitment. Self-awareness and creative use of self are preconditions for emotional engagement, which in turn provides the opportunity to foster hope and win emotional commitment. Winning spiritual commitment, however, is less of a linear affair. It requires a leader to create a kind of energy field, an atmosphere, which suffuses all of her attempts to win intellectual and emotional commitment. In order to win spiritual commit-

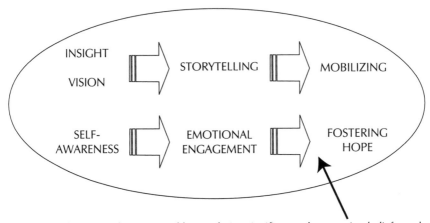

The atmosphere created by *rendering significance,* by *enacting beliefs,* and by *centering* inspires spiritual commitment while engaging in the processes of inspiring intellectual and emotional commitment

Figure Part 3-1. Winning spiritual commitment requires that a leader create an atmosphere that circumscribes all of his attempts to win intellectual and emotional commitment.

ment, a leader's insight, vision, story, and attempts to mobilize must be suffused with spirit. Spirit must also permeate his self-awareness, emotional engagement, and efforts to foster hope. This is shown in Figure Part 3-1.

Leaders who win spiritual commitment do not impose their efforts to do so upon their efforts to win intellectual and emotional commitment; rather, spirit is the ground on which those latter efforts rest. Winning spiritual commitment in an organization is not a matter of "bringing spirit into the workplace" or "implementing spirit." Spirit is already and inevitably on the premises. The CEO of a training and development company, a respected leader, was speaking to a Native American healer about his attempts to bring spirit to his company and to other organizations. This puzzled the Native American healer, who thought it preposterous to think that spirit was not present. "It may be suffering," said the healer, "but it is always present." A leader's role is not bringing spirit, but releasing and or healing it, and then offering it direction.

Spiritually committed people are "on a mission" that involves a long-term commitment to transform a community, which may be as large as human society itself or as small as a nuclear family.

9

Rendering Significance

I live my own life no longer, but the life of the living Whole.

—EDMOND GORE ALEXANDER HOLMES

leader who wishes to win the highest level of commitment—spiritual commitment—must be able to imbue her insight, vision, and story with what mythologist and author Joseph Campbell called *spiritual significance.* Writing about those who aspire to transform human life, Campbell noted, "the problem is nothing if not that of rendering the modern world spiritually significant—or rather (phrasing the same principle the other way round) nothing if not that of making it possible for men and women to come to full human maturity through the conditions of contemporary life."[1] This, then, is one task of modern leaders—rendering the current world spiritually significant, helping people come to full human maturity through the diverse forms of their individual lives.

In the modern world, where intellect, ego, and technology are primary objects of worship, the lines of communication have been severed between the realm of spirit, soul, and divine meaning and that of day-to-day existence and earthbound effort. *Rendering significance* involves helping followers reconnect those lines.

The task, of course, requires that leaders have found spiritual significance in their own lives. Doing so is not solely the product of a leader adhering to a religious doctrine or engaging in religious practices, but, says Campbell, having successfully completed the very complex "adventure of the hero." This adventure is one that everyone must take to become a fully mature person, even if that person never takes on the role of liberating society. It is particularly necessary, however, for those who would take on that role—for leaders.

The hero's adventure is a challenge or series of challenges, the completion of which allows the leader to bring her spiritual energies forward. Campbell wrote:

> The usual hero adventure begins with someone from whom something has been taken, or who feels something is lacking in the normal experiences available or permitted to the members of his society. This person then takes off on a series of adventures beyond the ordinary, either to recover what has been lost or to discover some life-giving elixir. It's usually a cycle, a going and a returning.[2]

The adventure is as much a spiritual and psychological internal journey as it is a meeting of the demands of external circumstances. As the hero slays the dragon, his internal dragon is also slain, and the hero is thus transformed by the adventure. The use of the term *hero* in the context of leadership does not mean that a leader must be viewed by others as a hero, or even that he behaves in a particularly heroic way. It means, rather, that the leader has attained maturity by virtue of meeting the challenge or enduring the suffering of the adventure while also completing a rite of passage into the world of the divine and back again, reentering to the human world and carrying a benefit—a godsend, a boon for mankind, a restorative elixir. This maturity then allows a leader to render significance to the supportive acts of followers, and to win spiritual commitment. If they fail to complete the adventure, then winning spiritual commitment to profound insights and noble visions will be beyond their reach. Campbell wrote that the hero "is the man or woman who has been able to battle past his personal and local historical limitations," and having done so, returns transfigured to society, ready to "teach the lesson he has learned of life renewed."[3]

Campbell and others have described the hero's adventure as it is told in ancient tales. The descriptions are rich and detailed, the adventure having many facets and many variations. There are four facets of the hero's adventure that are particularly salient for leaders who wish to win spiritual commitment: overcoming the trials placed before the hero, her submission of ego, discovering or retrieving the godsend, and the hero's subsequent ability to access two worlds—the world of everyday things and events, and the world of spirit.

Trials and Passion

Campbell wrote, "The trials are designed to see to it that the intending hero should be really a hero. Is he really a match for this task? Can he overcome the dangers? Does he have the courage, the knowledge, the capacity, to enable him to serve?"[4]

Can Lancelot meet the terrors of the Chapel Perilous at midnight? Can Theseus face the Minotaur? Can Luke Skywalker survive entering the Death Star? Can Alice Harris extricate herself and her infant children from poverty and homelessness on the streets of Watts? Can Zalman Schachter-Shalomi face the trepidation of approaching old age and overcome a temptation to yield to depression? Can Bill Strickland rise above adolescent aimlessness in the cauldron of a decaying neighborhood? Doing so, as Campbell pointed out, requires courage and knowledge. It also requires passion.

Some precision in definition is needed for understanding the fullness of the term *passion* because the term has many meanings and connotations. The word is most often used to refer to intense emotions such as love and hate, to strong sexual excitement, and to high enthusiasm. The last of those meanings is the one most often implied when senior-level people in an organization seek commitment, as in, "We need people to be passionate about our new vision." As it is used here, however, the term *passion* refers to something other than intense emotions or sexual excitement, and to something much more robust than high enthusiasm.

Here, the term *passion* carries with it a quality that some modern dictionaries consider archaic or obsolete: the quality of suffering or of enduring an ordeal. It is obvious that leaders must be passionate about their causes. Pat Croce made the point succinctly, "Passion is what fuels it." What is not so obvious is that such passion arises from having surpassed trials or endured suffering, and in the process having also reached into personal depths, thus effecting the transformation of the self. As Croce said, the trials, the suffering, can make those who endure them, "stronger when we pursue our goals and visions."

Once the trials are met and the passion has surfaced, life cannot be the same as it was. Lancelot becomes a Knight fit for the search for the Holy Grail. Theseus assumes his father's throne as King of Athens. Luke Skywalker becomes a Jedi Knight, Alice Harris becomes a messenger of hope, Zalman Schachter-Shalomi becomes a revered spiritual elder, and Bill Strickland becomes a champion of the power of believing in people. The deep-seated passion found on the adventure provides purpose to a life, simplifying it. Croce said, "I have to be passionate about something to keep my focus on the purpose. When you are passionate about something and you can feel it, smell it, taste it, and enjoy it, you will sacrifice some things that aren't as important." When a leader is passionate, his life becomes fine-tuned to fit the passion rather than the other way around. Bill Strickland said of his own life, "There are a thousand reasons I could give why this makes no sense; to spend a life this way. But the benefit is really the stuff that I believe in: kids, quality of life, and doing things the right way. That's why I get up in the morning."

Submission of Ego

A second facet of the hero's adventure that is significant for leaders is what Campbell called "the annihilation of the human ego."[5] This ego, he said, is "What you think you want, what you will to believe, what you think you can afford, what you decide to love, what you regard yourself as bound to."[6] All of this, all of the willful strivings are stripped away during the course of the hero's adventure.

The story of Michael Azzopardi, a Maltese Roman Catholic priest, is a rich expression of the annihilation of ego. During the early 1920s, the young Azzopardi studied law at Malta University, but switched to the study of theology when it became clear to him that he wanted to pursue his calling to the priesthood. In the late 1920s, he was given the opportunity to study at the Gregorian Institute in Rome. He saw this opportunity as a great honor, was thrilled to have it bestowed on him, and dreamed of the prestigious assignments that seemed sure to come his way after his graduation. He thought he was destined for greatness, and for a life of prestige and service. He was, but in no way that he could have imagined. Azzopardi was surprised and deeply disappointed when, after his studies in Rome were completed, he was ordered back to Malta in the role of a parish priest.[7]

He did not allow his dreams to die, deciding that, if he was to ever get the prestigious assignment he believed was surely his, he would have to be the best parish priest the Catholic Church had ever seen.

The years passed. He taught religion in a secondary school, and led retreats for teenagers. He acted as a chaplain during World War II. He chaired a committee to oversee the creation of a center of Catholic culture in Malta. He traveled the countryside visiting the sick and elderly. He went on radio with weekly broadcasts for those unable to attend mass, and with a show explaining each Sunday's gospel. In other words, he attended to business.

Azzopardi also made surprising and disturbing discoveries. He found mentally and physically challenged children hidden away by their families. There were children whose existence was unknown to neighbors, and children locked away during the day as their families worked in the fields or otherwise made a living. These children touched him deeply, as did the families who hid them away, and whose shame about having them was profound. He began to conceive of a home for the children, many of whom came from impoverished families. The children would be cared for and the families counseled.

On September 12, 1965, he spoke of this idea during a radio broadcast, "The Hour for the Sick." When he returned to his home, a young woman stood outside the door clutching an envelope. She had been waiting there for him for more than four hours. He approached her, and she told him that she had heard his radio appeal for a home for handicapped children. She reached out and offered the envelope to him, explaining that it contained money that she had been saving for a vacation. She was giving the money to him instead; to start, she said, "your home for the children."

Azzopardi knew that if he took that envelope his life would never be what he had expected it to be, and would never be the same as it had been. At that moment his life hung in the balance. There was a choice to be made. Should he, as Arthur did, pull the sword from the stone, he would reveal himself, and bear the weight of leadership. Is he up to the task at hand? Does he have the knowledge, the courage, and the passion to succeed? He must confront his own resistances and fears: until that moment he had not thought of the home as "his." He hesitated for an instant, deciding whether to commit himself, and then he took the envelope. It contained 100 Maltese pounds, about $300 dollars. He had been a parish priest for thirty years. He was fifty-five years old.

The moment of accepting the envelope is one of annihilating ego. What Azzopardi thought he wanted, what he willed himself to believe about his future, what he regarded himself as bound to—all of this fell away. He was bound instead to an elixir—an insight and a vision. His life was transformed. Campbell wrote, "If you realize what the real problem is—losing yourself, giving yourself to some higher end, or to another—you realize that this itself is the ultimate trial."[8] Even if the act of withdrawing the sword or accepting the envelope is not taken with full conscious awareness, even if it arises from a little-understood compulsion or obligation, when it is the right act, the only one that can be made with integrity, the soul knows what is being accepted.

The Godsend

Azzopardi's godsend, the reward for facing the deplorable situations of the challenged children of Malta, and of staring down his own resistance and ambition, was the insight that there should be no shame attached to such children. This is the treasure that he had unknowingly been seeking on his adventure, what Campbell called "the life-giving elixir." It gave new life to Azzopardi, to the children, to their families, and to an entire society.

Azzopardi's godsend now has a concrete reality. Today on Malta there stands a collection of buildings known as *Id-Dar tal-Provvidenza*—the House of Divine Providence. It consists of three villas, each housing a different age group of physically and mentally challenged children and adults. It is noted as one of the best homes of its kind in Europe. Azzopardi died in 1987, having devoted his last twenty-two years to what he fondly called his "angels"—the physically and mentally challenged residents of *Id-Dar tal-Provvidenza*. Many Maltese people think of him as a saint. After Azzopardi's death, his good friend, Lewis Portelli, wrote about him:

> Perhaps one of his greatest achievements . . . was his herculean feat in persuading parents and relatives to "take out" their handicapped, many times from the "hidden" places where they were kept. He was the one who convinced everyone that having a sick or handicapped member in the family was nothing to be ashamed of.[9]

The hero, then, is the person—man or woman—who has transcended both personal confines and the limits of her society. As a leader, the person who has set out upon her own particular adventure becomes what Deepak Chopra referred to as "the symbolic soul of the group," standing for the aspirations of individual followers to transform their own personal confines, and for the group's desire to transcend its collective limits.

Godsends come in many forms. When Lancelot does find the passion to meet the terrors of the Chapel Perilous at midnight, he returns with a sword and a shroud to heal a Knight of the Round Table. When Theseus slays the Minotaur he frees Greece from an annual sacrifice of seven youths and seven maidens. Luke Skywalker and his companions do survive the Death Star and rescue Princess Leia, giving new hope to those who are rebelling against the Empire. When Alice Harris does extricate herself and her infant children from poverty and homelessness on the streets of Watts she finds a loving god, overcomes her own self-damaging pride, and now tells us, "Don't ever be ashamed to ask for help." When Zalman Schachter-Shalomi faces the trepidation of approaching old age he returns from a sacred place where he performed sacred rituals. He now tells us, "Together, we will help give birth to a new civilization of unprecedented human development, spearheaded by spiritual elders working with people of all ages to create a peaceful and harmonious global society."[10] When Bill Strickland overcomes teenage aimlessness and the crumbling physical and social structures of his neighborhood he finds a spiritual practice in the art of pottery. He now says of those who make use of his organizations, "There is nothing wrong with the kids that come here except they don't have an opportunity to show that they are world-class citizens. You treat them that way and they will."

The insights such as those of Azzopardi, Harris, Schachter-Shalomi, and Strickland, are godsends, restorative benefits to society brought back by people who undertook the hero's journey. The godsend found on the adventure is not easily won; no great prize is ever easily won.

Access to Two Worlds

A third facet of the hero's adventure is also particularly significant for leaders: having returned to society bearing the elixir, the hero now has access to two worlds—the common world of the everyday, and the exceptional world of spirit and the unconscious. The leader who has completed the adventure is thus able to open the lines of communication between the two. This is another, yet quite different challenge, drawing once again upon the leader's passion. How to demonstrate the value of the captivating godsend to a society that welcomes only rationality, the bottom line, individual achievement, and the requirements of the self-centered ego? How to share the elixir with those who would become its champions without having it watered down, causing it to be superficial and ineffective? How to imbue workplaces with spirit without trivializing it as just another training event or a corporate flavor-of-the-month program? Campbell asked the question this way: "How represent on a two-dimensional surface a three-dimensional form, or in a three-dimensional image a multi-dimensional meaning?"[11] Doing so requires the artistry of leadership.

One avenue to finding answers to all of the questions above is to become a founder, to build an institution from the bottom up. Alice Harris founded Parents of Watts. Zalman Schachter-Shalomi founded the Spiritual Eldering Institute. Dale Fushek founded Life Teen. Bill Strickland founded Manchester Craftsman's Guild. Founders have certain advantages, chief among them being the opportunity to determine what gets talked about, how things get done, and who does them. Still, funds must be solicited, permits obtained, and certifications won, all of which require the grounding of a godsend. Another avenue is to take the reins of an organization in which it is clear to everyone concerned (or at least almost everyone) that the elixir is needed. This is the route Pat Croce chose when he became president of the Philadelphia 76ers. Still, a general manager and a coach had to be replaced, fans won over, the right players signed. The third and most difficult route is to offer the elixir where it poses a serious threat to a well-defended status quo and is thus unwelcome. Succeeding at this task places leaders in the realm of highest jeopardy and greatest potential effect. Leaders such as Jesus, Nelson Mandela, Martin Luther King, and Mohandas Gandhi come to mind as those who have succeeded on this most perilous route.

No matter the route, however, those who succeed at winning spiritual commitment will still be leaders—they will have mastered the arts of winning intellectual, emotional, and spiritual commitment. We have almost come full circle, back to the beginning of this book, back to considering the competencies for winning intellectual commitment—insight, vision, storytelling, and mobilizing—and those for winning emotional commitment—self-awareness, emotional engagement, and fostering hope. If a leader can bring to those competencies the spiritual maturity that is born out of the hero's adventure, he can render significance of the highest order—spiritual significance.

Spiritual significance shows up in noble visions such as those discussed in Chapter 3: in Jim Wold's vision, *improving teaching and learning so all students achieve high standards of performance*; in Bloorview Mac-Millan's vision, *defy disability*; in the vision of Fielding Graduate Institute, *a collaborative family of scholar-practitioners, empowered by a global perspective, enabling and promoting harmony and social justice*; in NEC's vision to *promote an exchange of information and knowledge for the achievement of a new creativity in society*; and in the vision of Fujita, *a world that combines a rich natural environment and vibrant societies with caring communities*.

A spiritually mature leader will uncover an insight with depth of meaning (a godsend), will craft a noble vision communicating that depth, will tell his story of change in a soulful way, including the trials and the suffering, and will mobilize people by connecting their everyday actions to lofty purposes. His self-awareness will circumscribe and contain spiritual awareness as well as emotional awareness. Emotional engagement will include speaking of the leader's feelings about the joys and perils of his adventure, and the adventure that the leader and followers are completing together. The spiritually mature leader will foster hope, not only for the people who follow, but also for some larger community or society. In short, a spiritually mature leader will bring that maturity to everything he does in a public way, rendering significance to his endeavors and winning spiritual commitment.

Development Strategies for Rendering Significance

Perhaps it is oxymoronic to speak of "strategies" and "spiritual significance" together because a leader's ability to render spiritual significance depends upon her consciousness of spiritual matters and not upon any particular plan or design. Still, there is useful advice to be given, even if that advice requires a certain consciousness in order for it to prove useful, and even if that advice contains a warning that the leader must embrace a spiritual perspective before anyone else will offer spiritual commitment. The useful advice to leaders, then, is to recognize their own depth, to uncover the moral and honorable reasons why anyone ought to commit to their insights and visions, and to be generous about sharing the circumstances and challenges of their own hero's adventures.

Following Your Bliss

Joseph Campbell advised, "Follow your bliss." That advice has sometimes been misinterpreted to mean that we are to do whatever we feel like doing, but Campbell had something else in mind. He meant discovering what makes us happy, "not excited, nor just thrilled, but deeply happy."[12] Campbell's bliss is beyond the happiness that we feel when things are going well for us. It comes out of a deeper appreciation for the meaning of what we are doing, and exists even when things are not going well for us. We can be happy and blissful, and that is certainly the preferred state, but we can also be unhappy and blissful when we are consciously connected to the depth of meaning that has brought the circumstances of our unhappiness upon us. The latter state is what is meant by the term *passion*.

This discovery of one's bliss is not a product of intellectual analysis, but the result of going, "where your body and soul want to go."[13] Not where you think you should go, not where you hoped to go. When Michael Azzopardi accepted the envelope from the woman who stood waiting in front of his home, he went where his body and soul wanted to go. Campbell wrote:

> . . . if you do follow your bliss, you put yourself on a kind of track that has been there all the while, waiting for you, and the life you ought to be living is the one you are living.[14]

A leader who wishes to win spiritual commitment in others must first find and follow his bliss. The leader who does so is then capable of bringing spiritual energy into the drama of creating significant change.

Uncovering a Moral Objective

Spiritual commitment attaches only to aims that those who make the commitment view as being moral and honorable, such as aims to revive or transform a society, or another human being, or a single idea, or the content of consciousness. Wesley Clark provided an example of a moral and honorable aim, while also acknowledging that such aims are sometimes difficult to uncover. He said, "The moral component is more clear-cut in the military because you can say that you are doing this for the country and it is the right thing to do."

This is the essence of what was called *noble vision* in Chapter 3—the vision is about much more than self-interest. Where leaders cannot find moral and honorable aims, spiritual commitment will not show up. Clark said it this way, "You have to have a moral and ethical component to leadership. You have to believe in it. You have to give people an incentive, a thrill, a sense of accomplishment—but there is something deeper than that."

Creating a Sacred Autobiography

In his book, *Soul Prints*, Marc Gafni, who is dean of Melitz Public Culture Center, urges that we each should create our sacred autobiography. He wrote, "We need to know that in the details of our lives dangle the keys to heaven."[15] A sacred autobiography sheds light on the meaning of a life, connecting the daily details with the being of the soul, and with our best understanding of the texture of human and divine existence. Our sacred autobiographies, says Gafni, ought to be told to others.

Gafni's suggestion is especially imperative for leaders who wish to win the highest levels of commitment. A leader's sacred autobiography becomes her personal narrative, part of the story that is related, along with the godsend of a compelling insight and the grounding of that insight in a noble vision.

There is a certain vulnerability attached to this telling; a bearing of the soul that may also be laden with deep emotion. A leader who does decide to tell of his personal inner adventure needs to be prepared to engage emotionally with followers because the story will stir the emotions. When the story is told well, told with honesty and sincerity, and told frequently, the telling affords a leader the opportunity to win all levels of commitment—intellectual, emotional, and spiritual.

Summary

Rendering significance is one of three leadership competencies for winning spiritual commitment. It is the means through which leaders communicate the spiritual depth of their insights and visions, and enable people to develop maturity as spiritual beings. A leader's ability to render significance is a direct function of having found spiritual meaning in her life. This meaning flows from enduring and profiting from the trials of the leader's particular life, finding something of value to others, sharing that something freely, and developing the ability to draw the connecting lines between the spiritual and the everyday.

• • •

Questions About Yourself to Contemplate or Discuss with Others

Who, in your life experience, was practiced at rendering significance?

To what degree are you practiced at rendering significance?

What is it about rendering significance that rings true for your current leadership role?

How important is rendering significance to your further development as a leader?

Notes

1. Joseph Campbell, *The Hero with a Thousand Faces* (N.J.: Princeton University Press, 1973): 388.
2. Joseph Campbell with Bill Moyers, *The Power of Myth* (N.Y.: Anchor Books, 1988): 152.
3. Campbell, *The Hero with a Thousand Faces*, 20.
4. Campbell, *The Power of Myth*, 14.
5. Campbell, *The Hero with a Thousand Faces*, 390.
6. Campbell, *The Power of Myth*, 184.
7. The story of Michael Azzopardi's life is drawn from interviews and discussions with Lewis Portelli, Sylvia Ear, and Achille Mizzi, and from the Web site of *Id-Dar tal-Provvidenza* <http://www.dar-tal-providenza.org>, and from Lewis Portelli, "Mgr. Michael Azzopardi: An Appreciation by Lewis Portelli," *The Sunday Times* (Malta, May 31, 1987).
8. Campbell, *The Power of Myth*, 154.
9. Portelli, "Mgr. Michael Azzopardi: An Appreciation by Lewis Portelli."
10. Zalman Schachter-Shalomi and Ronald S. Miller, *From Age-ing to Sage-ing: A Profound New Vision of Growing Older* (N.Y.: Warner Books, 1995): 8.
11. Campbell, *The Hero with a Thousand Faces*, 218.
12. Campbell, *The Power of Myth*, 193.
13. Ibid., 147.
14. Ibid., 150.
15. Marc Gafni, *Soul Prints: Your Path to Fulfillment* (N.Y.: Pocket Books, 2001): 232.

10

Enacting Beliefs

It is not so much what you believe in that matters, as the way in which you believe it and proceed to translate that belief into action.

— LIN YUTANG

he challenge is confronted by every religion, by every political body, by every organization that espouses a set of values or operating principles, by every culture, by most people, and by every effective leader: How to translate beliefs into actions. Our beliefs are the fundamental ground of the judgments we make about ourselves, others, and the events of our lives, and thus they hold sway over our behavior. For example, if we believe that people are basically good, we are likely to treat them with respect and dignity. And if we believe they are basically selfish and untrustworthy, we are likely to treat them with caution and suspicion.

Beliefs are not knowledge but articles of faith; either we need no proof of their truth, or our perceptions are constructed in such a way that their truth is continually proven to us. They are our personal certainties, sometimes borrowed from others, changeable over time and with experience. For as long as we hold beliefs, though, they are highly resistant, perhaps even immune to persuasion of their falseness.

In previous chapters we have seen many examples of how leaders succeed at the important challenge of translating beliefs into action. Zalman Schachter-Shalomi believes that, "People . . . become wise by undertaking the inner work that leads in stages to expanded consciousness."[1] He translated that belief into action by both immersing himself in a retreat to discover the source of his unease over growing older and by founding the Spiritual Eldering Institute. Dale Fushek believes in the power of love, so he founded Life Teen, Inc. Mary Ellen Hennen believed the people she inherited when she became executive director of the Public Utilities Commission of Minnesota were capable and well positioned to make a difference, so she turned them loose to solve an intractable problem. Pat Croce, Beverly O'Neill, Alice Harris, Wilma Mankiller, Bill Strickland, and every other leader who wins high commitment, believe in the efficacy of optimism, so they express and maintain their own.

We have also seen, in recent times, the abject failure of organizations to enact their beliefs. For example, the values espoused by Enron in its *1998 Annual Report* are, *respect, integrity, communication,* and *excellence.* In describing *respect,* the report stated, "Ruthlessness, callousness, and arrogance don't belong here."[2]

Leaders and Beliefs

Leaders are often reluctant to explicitly bring their beliefs to their leadership unless, like Monsignor Dale Fushek or Rabbi Zalman Schachter-Shalomi, they lead within a religious context; unless they "wear the cloth" of priest or nun, rabbi, minister, or imam, or they hold some other designation as a consecrated person of religious stature. Many leaders outside of a religious context are justifiably anxious that explicitly bringing their particular brand of beliefs forward in a multireligious society will cause unnecessary and unproductive conflict. Still, whether leaders wear the cloth of their faith or not, those who win high commitment do enact their beliefs.

The second of the three competencies for winning spiritual commitment, *enacting beliefs* does not necessarily mean explicitly bringing a set of religious beliefs, or a particular religion, forward. It means, rather, actively employing deeply held beliefs in the general course of leadership. There is a key test involved: *Is a particular action intended primarily as a religious statement?* For those who lead outside a religious context, enacting beliefs is never intended as a religious statement. It is intended, rather, to provide leadership and to win commitment from others in a way that preserves personal integrity. For leaders who are clearly leading within a religious context the action may be both an attempt to win commitment and a religious statement as well.

Beliefs in Practice

A leader who enacts her beliefs achieves a close integration—a coming together—of beliefs and actions. Vincent Francia is a good example. Francia, after serving four years on the Town Council of Cave Creek, Arizona, has been elected mayor three times. Cave Creek prides itself on being, "The Town Too Tough to Govern." Francia says, "It is an accurate description of the citizenry of the town; an eclectic mix of people that take democracy very seriously. Everyone is expected to voice their opinion. They don't accept being governed, but do accept guidance." The town has been hard on its elected officials; one mayor was recalled, and in the 2003 election, the citizen's of Cave Creek rejected the city's new general plan, a very rare occurrence. When asked why he has been successful as the town's mayor, Francia replied, "I keep the peace and can hold things together in the worst of times."

Francia's ability to hold things together begins with enacting his beliefs; in his case, Buddhist tenets and practices. For example, he makes use of the Buddhist practice of *mindful listening*. "I don't make judgments about what you are saying," he explained. "I am the one who can sit in the middle and get along with all groups. I keep the peace. When you are practicing mindful listening you are like the emptiness in a vase, and that vase can hold anything. Whatever you have to say, it is going to be received. It is not going to be taken casually or be dismissed." Mindful listening breeds trust, which in turn breeds loyalty.

Francia provided a brief overview of Buddhist philosophy and practice while offering examples of how he enacts his beliefs in the political arena. Buddha, says Francia, focused on the question of why human beings suffer, and on what might be done to alleviate that suffering. The first two of Buddha's Four Noble Truths are, in brief, that everybody everywhere suffers, and that the source of suffering is desire. Francia said, "If you take these two concepts and translate them into a political arena, they have quite a bit of application." Francia cites the example of a citizen who is trying to get something done, fails, and suffers because she did not get what was desired.

In his third noble truth, Buddha explores the cause of suffering, believing that which has a cause also has a cure. The cause of suffering is a sense of separation, the sense of "I" as a separate entity. Western psychology refers to it as ego. Francia said, "A healthy ego is fine. But when it causes separation—male from female, Republican from Democrat, environmentalist from private property rights person—then what has been created is conflict." Conflict is a source of suffering.

As a solution to suffering, the Buddha put forth an Eightfold Path in his fourth noble truth so that in the course of living we do not have to live a life of suffering.[3] One aspect of the Eightfold Path is Right Speech, which depends on the realization that saying unkind or cruel things has negative consequences; it causes suffering. Francia said, "In terms of political application, if I am practicing mindful listening, the next step is to speak. Buddhism holds that when you speak to a person, you do so to encourage or to bring joy."

"If I strike out," said Francia, "The effect of my statement is that it has discounted what the person said. It has embarrassed him in front of his elected officials, and probably humiliated him in front of his fellow citizens." Doing so can create a chain reaction that brings more suffering to more people. Francia's Buddhist beliefs provide him with an alternative to striking out: "If, on the other hand, I speak to him in a way that is encouraging, even though I may not be able to vote for what he wishes, and in a way that brings joy and that thanks him for bringing this to the council's attention, then he has been heard and that which he has been saying has been respected."

Francia is not explicitly bringing his Buddhist faith forward. He is, rather, consciously employing his beliefs and practices—in this particular example, mindful listening and right speech—in the general course of his leadership role. He has no intention of making a religious statement. Rather, his intention is to be a leader that provides a fractious community with a sense of peace and an atmosphere of mutual respect upon which it can build its future.

Francia also can be seen performing subtle movements with his hands, called *mudras*. These are symbolic gestures that are intended to help him shift his consciousness. A *mudra* enables him to respond to difficult situations in ways that encourage joy.

Enacting beliefs is, of course, not solely the province of Buddhists, and beliefs themselves are not solely the province of the world's formal religions. For example, Wilma Mankiller's unflagging optimism is an enactment of traditional Cherokee beliefs: *first let us remove all negative things from our mind so we can come together as one*. And Jim Ellis, as a U.S. Army officer, pledged an oath to support and defend the Constitution of the United States. He carries a copy of it in his briefcase as both a reminder of his oath and as a set of principles to live and lead by. This adherence to beliefs, this close integration of belief and action, is the basis of integrity.

The specific ways in which leaders enact their beliefs vary from leader to leader and from belief to belief. Certain beliefs, however, are held in common among leaders who are able to win high levels of commitment:

- Belief in divine involvement in the affairs of the world
- Belief in the importance of service
- Belief in the basic goodness of people

These three beliefs lead human beings closer to soul, and thus open the door for spiritual commitment. United with the willingness and ability to enact them, these beliefs separate leaders who win high levels of commitment from those who are simply supermanagers.

Divine Involvement

The first belief held in common by leaders who win high commitment was expressed by Pat Croce, by Bonnie Wright, and by many other leaders as well. Croce said, "My undying tenet is that if you do your best, God will take care of the rest." Wright said it this way, adding a small but important twist to Croce's words: "If you are doing the right things, the resources are going to come to you to do it." The statements of Croce and Wright, when combined, form a summary of what leaders generally express when talking about divine involvement: When you are doing the right things, and when you are doing them to the best of your ability, the divine powers of the universe will accomplish whatever else is needed.

This belief in divine involvement is also a source of strength and renewal for leaders. Croce's belief that if he does his best God will take care of the rest provides him with a basis for dealing with the inevitable problems that all leaders face. With that belief in hand, he said, "You then can handle setbacks, disappointments, and frustrations." Beverly O'Neill expressed a similar outlook when she said, "I know there is a higher power. I have defined it myself in my own way. The strength sustains me."

The Primacy of Service

The second belief that is common among leaders who win high levels of commitment is belief in the importance of living a life of service. Wilma Mankiller, for example, said that she initially ran for the office of chief of the Cherokee Nation because she wanted to be in a position to allocate more resources to very rural and poor people.

Alice Harris, speaking about the many organizations she has founded and headed said, "I don't lay out agendas. Whatever people's needs are, we are going to take care of them. Whether it is getting them to the welfare office or the White House, they are going to get there because that is what the need is." Harris is direct and fierce about the matter of service. "We should be helping all the time," she said. "We have to come out of our own comfort zone and start helping people."

David Hollister also has the needs of people in the forefront of his leadership. Hollister said, "Some people go into public life and you know that it is self-serving. That is not something that has ever interested me. I could have taken different jobs and made a hell of a lot more money. But I deeply believe in public service." When Hollister was in the Michigan legislature he was asked to take responsibility for the state's social service budget. He was warned that if he accepted the responsibility, he could, in his words, "Kiss off any ambition to ever be governor or have any state-wide role." Effectiveness at managing the social service budget was likely to alienate many of the state's power brokers. Hollister said, "I took on that task with a great deal of enthusiasm." He traveled the state organizing people around basic issues such as hunger and homelessness. During his tenure in Michigan state government, Hollister was consistently ranked among the state's top legislators. He eventually did gain the state-wide role that he was warned would never be his, heading one of the most influential departments in the Michigan state government.

The commitment to service for leaders such as Mankiller, Harris, and Hollister is not mere political commitment. They do not serve for any other reason except to serve; they are not drawn to serve because it will be profitable or will insure the loyalty of others. They do it for its own sake and for its own rewards. Alice Harris said, "God loves a joyful giver." For leaders such as these, service is a spiritual commitment that wins spiritual commitment from others.

The zeal to serve is at the root of the compelling insights that give rise to noble visions. The insights that compel leaders are perceptions about the needs or aspirations of a group of people; they come out of belief in the primacy of service. Noble visions are about the specific contributions that leaders intend to make to a group of people; they too have their roots in the impulse to serve and they invite followers to serve as well. Without this impulse to serve, without this belief in the primacy of service, compelling insights and noble visions elude would-be leaders. Alice Harris expressed a wish for all of us that also conveyed an important message to leaders when she said, "If we could just come to the knowledge that giving is *the* end."

Philosopher and theologian Sam Keen eloquently expressed the significance of believing in the primacy of service. He wrote:

Whenever you are confused, keep heading in the direction that leads toward deepening your love and care for all living beings, including yourself, and you will never stray far from the path to fulfillment.[4]

The Goodness of People

The third belief that is common among leaders who win high levels of commitment is belief in the basic goodness of others. Despite declarations to the contrary, our institutions and many people who hold leadership positions tend to operate as if people are basically selfish, needing to be watched and scrutinized carefully to prevent rampant and destructive self-interest. However, leaders who win high levels of commitment conduct themselves in just the opposite way, as if people are basically unselfish, and as if they are trustworthy.

Belief in the basic goodness of others has lurked as a subtext in much of what has been said in previous chapters, and its presence now requires full acknowledgement. For example, Pat Croce said, "I am a big believer in people." Bill Strickland said, "There is nothing wrong with the kids that come here, except that they don't have an opportunity to show that they are world-class citizens." And one of Bonnie Wright's rules for leadership is, "Look for the wisdom in the group." Croce, Strickland, and Wright were each affirming their belief in the goodness of others. Such statements are not simply about the capabilities of others, but about the basic nature of human beings.

This belief is what invitational theorists refer to as the assumption of *trust*. William Purkey described the assumption of trust in this way: "Given an optimally inviting environment, each person will find his or her own best ways of being and becoming."[5] Leaders who win high levels of commitment are adept at creating such optimally inviting environments, which depend heavily on the leader's willingness and ability to hold onto the assumption of trust.

Beliefs and Values

A leader's own beliefs are entwined with but independent from those of whatever organization he leads, unless that organization is small and the leader is also the founder. Organizational leaders often attempt to articulate beliefs for their organizations in what has come to be called a *values statement*. However, like many vision statements, values statements can depreciate rapidly into hollow words printed on wall posters, mouse pads, and coffee mugs. This depreciation happens for one or both of two reasons. First, it happens when those in leadership positions fail to recognize what they really do value, opting instead for statements about what they think their organization ought to value, or about what they think the organization ought to be seen as valuing by its employees, customers, and other stakeholders. The result is values statements containing words such as *trust* and *respect*, accompanied by actions that shout out that the actual and primary values are those such as *achievement, competition, status,* and *wealth.* There is nothing wrong with valuing such things as achievement, competition, status, and wealth. But anyone who wishes to win commitment from others needs to own up to what they really value rather than pretending to value whatever they believe will play well in the marketplace for commitment.

Second, the depreciation of a values statement happens when those in leadership positions fail to institutionalize the values that their organizations espouse, opting for a communication campaign alone as the means to proclaim and ground what they say they believe in and care about. Organizational leaders, as a whole, do know how to institutionalize a value. *Safety,* for example, is well enshrined in organizations where it has been made a high priority. Those who do institutionalize safety know that communication must be relentless, and that it must be accompanied by training and monitoring. So the consistent and pervasive failure to institutionalize values is not a matter of not knowing how; it is more a function of not caring all that much about the stated values in the first place, or of assuming people will know what is meant by the words on the poster, mouse pad, or coffee cup without a great deal of dialogue and feedback.

Leaders who wish to create a statement of beliefs or values for their organizations have much the same choices for doing so as they do for creating a vision statement. They can articulate the beliefs or values, stand as the primary spokesperson and symbol for them, and then work to involve others. They can facilitate a group process to articulate the beliefs or values, opening up the possibility that others will take ownership early on, and risking that, in trying to please everyone involved, they "lose the juice." They can adopt beliefs and values that have been previously articulated, putting their own stamp on implementation.

No matter which choice a leader makes about how to identify and articulate beliefs and values, she cannot drift into the position where her personal beliefs and values fail to align with those that are eventually espoused. Doing so courts disaster. Leaders who win high levels of commitment know what they believe in and value, don't pretend to anything else, and persist in all ways possible on institutionalizing the beliefs that they hold dear and the values that they prize most highly.

Development Strategies for Enacting Beliefs

A leader's ability to enact his beliefs presumes that significant beliefs have been identified and acknowledged, that they can be articulated, and that some formal or informal mechanism has been created to test actions against beliefs.

Articulating Beliefs

In this chapter, three beliefs that are held in common among leaders who are able to win high levels of commitment were identified: belief in divine involvement in the affairs of the world, belief in the importance of service, and belief in the basic goodness of people. Other beliefs that drove the actions of specific leaders were also identified. For example, Zalman Schachter-Shalomi's belief that, "People . . . become wise by undertaking the inner work that leads in stages to expanded consciousness,"[6] Dale Fushek's belief in the power of love, and Vincent Francia's belief in his Buddhist practices.

Leaders who win high levels of commitment can articulate their beliefs, even if only to themselves. Bonnie Wright has a list of beliefs specifically about how she can best conduct herself as a leader. It includes items such as these: seek the wisdom of the group, operate from a position of love, be willing to be surprised, be bold, and be brave.

Connecting Actions with Beliefs

Having articulated their most deeply held beliefs, leaders who win high levels of commitment consciously test their actions and potential actions against their beliefs. This is detective work that may be accomplished as inwardly as in meditation or reflection, or as outwardly as in dialogue with trusted others who will offer feedback. There will be more to say about such feedback in the next chapter.

Choosing a Process

The "Development Strategies for Vision" section of Chapter 3 contains a more complete discussion of the alternatives in front of any leader who wishes to create an organization vision statement. Much of what is written there applies also to creating a statement of beliefs or values. In short, leaders have the option of articulating a belief or values themselves, steering a group process to articulate them, allowing them to emerge, or adopting them from someone else. Each alternative has advantages and disadvantages.

Summary

Leaders who win the highest levels of commitment actively employ their own deeply held beliefs in the course of their lives and their leadership roles. While they vary in their beliefs and in the specific ways in which they enact their beliefs, certain beliefs are common among them: belief in divine involvement in the affairs of the world, belief in the importance of service, and belief in the basic goodness of people. Leaders who win high levels of commitment know what they believe in and value, they don't pretend to anything else, and they are persistent about bringing their beliefs to the organizations they lead.

· · ·

Questions About Yourself to Contemplate or Discuss with Others

Who, in your life experience, was practiced at enacting beliefs?

To what degree are you practiced at enacting beliefs?

What is it about enacting beliefs that rings true for your current leadership role?

How important is enacting beliefs to your further development as a leader?

Notes

1. Zalman Schachter-Shalomi and Ronald S. Miller, *From Age-ing to Sage-ing: A Profound New Vision of Growing Older* (N.Y.: Warner Books, 1995): 15.
2. Enron, "Enron Annual Report 1998. Our Values," <http://www.enron.com/corp/investors/annuals/annual98/ourvalues.html> (June, 2003).
3. Background for the discussion of Buddhism is from <http://www.buddhanet.net> (June, 2003).
4. Sam Keen, *Hymns to an Unknown God: Awakening the Spirit in Everyday Life* (N.Y.: Bantam Books, 1994): 59.
5. William W. Purkey, "An Introduction to Invitational Theory," at *International Alliance for Invitational Education*, <http://www.invitationaleducation.net> (June, 2003).
6. Schachter-Shalomi and Miller, *From Age-ing to Sage-ing*, 15.

11

Centering

These are days when no one should rely unduly on his "competence." Strength lies in improvisation.

—WALTER BENJAMIN

A book is a linear creature; pages march forward from the first to
the final, demanding some measure of logic and order. A book
also impels its author to adopt a reductionist mind-set; topics
are separated into chapters which are further separated into sections. This
book, for example, contains a set of chapters, each describing a leadership
competency. The result of this linearity and reductionism may be the
erroneous conclusion that each competency is truly a discrete phenomenon.

The reality of commitment is, however, much more complex than a
set of discrete competencies. Mind, emotions, and spirit are aspects of a
single person, and winning minds, emotions, and spirits are inextricably

intertwined. A story, which is the food of the mind, emotion, which is the product of feeling, and soul, which drives spirit, all interact with and influence one another in ways that are little understood. In order to win the mind, emotion, and spirit of a single person a leader must have equal facility with all three, and be able to distinguish when each is called for. In this way a leader connects with others at every level of being. In other words, winning mind, emotion, and spirit must be approached in an integrated way; in a way that respects all three and treats them as a whole.

The Discipline of Bringing In

The intertwined nature of intellectual, emotional, and spiritual commitment requires the leader who wishes to win all three to be capable of what M. C. Richards calls "Centering . . . the discipline of bringing in rather than of leaving out."[1] In a leader's extended and ongoing dialogue with others, when the mind shows up, it must be brought in. When emotion shows up, it must be brought in. When spirit shows up, it too must be brought in. In order for each of them to show up, they must, of course, be invited. Leaders issue the invitations: Come to the party, bring all of yourself.

For Richards, centering is an activity of consciousness. It is not a state of being but a process and a discipline in which a person—an artist, a leader, anyone—engages from moment to moment with his experience, both inner and outer experience. In pottery, Richards describes it like this:

> For in centering the clay on the potter's wheel, one centers down . . . and then one immediately centers up. Down and up, wide and narrow, letting focus bear within it an expanding consciousness and letting a widened awareness . . . have the commitment to detail of a focused attention. Not "either . . . or," but "both . . . and."[2]

For a potter, it is not "either up or down," but "both up and down." Not "either widened awareness or commitment to detail" but "both widened awareness and commitment to detail." Centering entails transcending apparent opposites, finding the unity that lives within difference. For leaders who win high commitment, it is not "mind or emotion or spirit," but "mind and emotion and spirit." For leaders, centering incorporates the ability to bond compelling insights and lofty visions with everyday reality, to connect values with deeds, and to align their own efforts with a larger concern. Centering is integrity in action. Richards continued,

> You can perhaps feel the inner movement of a Centering consciousness that plays dramatically in the tides of inner and outer, self and other, in an instinctive hope towards wholeness.[3]

The centering consciousness of a leader seeks wholeness while playing in the tides of inner and outer, self and other, in the merging seas of mind, emotion, and spirit.

A Leader at Work

The following tale shows how a leader employs the leadership competencies for winning intellectual, emotional, and spiritual commitment while playing in those merging seas. The tale is based on real incidents.

> *Nearly 200 people gather in one large room for a daylong corporate meeting. As they enter the room, each of them finds a seat at one of twenty-five round tables, seven or eight people per table. While they mill and get settled, an executive of the company, the "host" of the meeting, roams around the room. He shakes hands, learns names, greets old acquaintances, and gets a sense of who is present.*
>
> *This does not look or feel like a typical corporate get-together; there is no imposing stage, very few suits and ties, no podium, and*

no one is preparing for a formal presentation. When everyone is seated and the meeting begins, the executive, dressed casually and with notes in hand, stands on a low platform at the long side of the rectangular room: the closest tables are just a few feet away. The low platform and nearby tables suggest intimacy between the executive and everyone else. He will often leave the platform in the course of this day and get even closer to the participants, occasionally joining them in discussions or simply observing them at work.

The executive leader for this meeting has become convinced that the traditional approach to such events does not produce results. He has addressed and attended many such traditional meetings, where someone stands at the front of the room, with a laser pointer in hand and a PowerPoint presentation at the ready. Minds may sometimes be convinced at such meetings, but emotions are rarely won, and there is almost never a true call to spirit. The more casual setting in this room, the proximity of the executive to the participants, and his willingness to "join the crowd" encourage rapport and dialogue, providing opportunities for everyone to be more authentic with one another than they normally are. These are all initial steps toward winning higher levels of commitment than the usual intellectual commitment.

Storytelling

The company sponsoring this meeting is an established and conventional insurance company that aspires to provide a broader range of financial services. Fulfilling this aspiration will necessitate higher levels of cooperation between divisions and departments, the sharing of information which had previously been held as sacrosanct and secret, and a greater measure of respect between groups. The participants are led through a series of experiences to help them understand the complex, competitive, and dynamic industry their company inhabits, to inform them about how the company makes money, and about how the company plans to respond to its new environment; this is the story the leader is telling. After the first such experience the participants have many questions. "How did we become so unresponsive to the outside world?" "Are we really as bad as it seems?" "What must we do?"

The people in the room were confronted with sobering data about the changing demographics, expectations and spending habits of their customers, about their company's market position, and about their performance relative to competitors. The total picture was not pretty—but it was an accurate story. The leadership of the organization wanted to engage the minds of its people by providing them with the very information that executives had when they created the company's new vision and strategy. In other words, the information was highly relevant, presented cogently and unforgettably, and everybody got the message. Interactive media encouraged mutual learning and dialogue between people from different slices of the organization. The information was shared in a way that allowed the people in the room to draw their own conclusions because people are more likely to act with conviction on their own conclusions rather than on someone else's. In this situation the conclusion was inescapable: We must change.

Drawing one's own conclusions is a particularly significant aspect of winning minds because as the mind reaches a conclusion the heart is often touched as well. One of the reasons that typical executive-up-front, PowerPoint presentations fail to produce results is that attendees are expected to understand and act on someone else's conclusions. In the meeting we are attending here, however, both minds and emotions are being won.

Insight and Self-Awareness

During a question and answer period the executive tells the group how he feels about the company's poor customer service. He speaks about measures of customer satisfaction, which are grim; he also speaks very personally about the hopes and dreams of customers, about the company's promises to them, and about his own deep disappointment in the company's failures. He is not haranguing the audience, but is simply and eloquently talking about himself—about his feelings for customers. There is not a sound in the room except for his voice. When he finishes, the entire room full of people seems to hesitate, stunned into silence, not quite believing that an executive of the firm cares in a heartfelt way about service and is willing to say so in such a public way. After this moment passes, a moment during which he scans the room nervously for some reaction, the room erupts in applause.

This executive was expected to deliver an urgent message. The message, honed in the company's headquarters, went something like this: "We are not doing well. The competition is passing us. We have lost sight of our customers; we have squandered their trust and must reclaim it. We have an opportunity to offer a broader range of services. We have to stop obsessing over our internal skirmishes, pull together, and make things work for the people we serve. We have little time: We must act now."

Prior to the meeting he told a trusted advisor, "I cannot fathom how we lost sight of the fact that what we do is help our customers fulfill their dreams. That is what we are supposed to do. We are supposed to help people fulfill their dreams. Their financial dreams, at least. That is what our customers expect of us. It is why they pay us."

The way he spoke of his feelings, a message from him rather than from headquarters, was qualitatively different from the way in which he talked about the message he was expected to deliver. It is not that the message from headquarters was wrong, but that his own message came from his heart rather than from the pages of talking points he was given. His tone of voice was both more thoughtful and more passionate, resonating from who he is as a person. After some discussion and encouragement from his advisor, he decided to talk during the meeting about what he felt. His concept about helping people fulfill their dreams is the insight that will drive his own work to transform the company.

What he did during the meeting was difficult and courageous for him—he spoke of his own emotions. He then decided to make creative use of his own feelings to engage more fully with his audience. Like most executives he is quite comfortable with and good at logical discourse, and quite good at following a script. He had always assumed that convincing people—winning minds—was enough. He is learning that, in order to effect fundamental change in his organization, winning intellectual commitment will not be enough. He will have to also win emotional and perhaps spiritual commitment. In order to do so, he must authentically share what is in his own heart, and what his own spirit is called to do.

Emotional Engagement and Fostering Hope

A man in the audience says, "I am so angry and frustrated! How on earth did this company fall so far? I had no idea things were this bad. And I am afraid that we will never get back to what we once were, let alone compete in this new market. It is clear that we got lazy and arrogant at the same time. Can we really fix this?"

The man is responding to a question from the executive leader, who had asked the group, "How do you feel about what you are learning today?"

After hearing the man's plea, the executive pauses for a moment, and then responds. "I feel pretty much the same way you do: sometimes angry and frustrated, and sometimes fearful. The job ahead of us is daunting, and we never should have gotten to this place at all. That part really ticks me off. How many of you feel the same way?"

The vast majority of people in the audience raise their hands.

"I don't mean to deny the importance of all the negatives," he continues. "But there are also many positives. Our company has

new leadership that understands how important it is for us to talk together like this. We have a huge customer base. Some pieces of the business are doing well. We have sold off some pieces that we never should have had in the first place. None of our competitors has really figured it all out yet either. We are building the right technology. So we have a good start. The rest is up to what we all do next—after we leave this room."

The executive's public declaration of his own frustration and disappointment—"I cannot fathom how we lost sight of the fact that what we do is help our customers fulfill their dreams"—is an invitation to others in the room to bring their feelings to the dialogue. The tide of the meeting shifts from the storytelling of the mind to the sea of emotion. The executive understands that gaining emotional commitment is a matter of acknowledging and valuing emotions of all kinds because individual emotions cannot be neatly separated but are bound to one another in a complex stew of feelings. He knows that if he wants to win the energy of enthusiasm or passion, he must also acknowledge and accept the energy of anger, frustration, and other less comfortable and less constructive feelings.

This executive also connects—heart-to-heart, empathetically—with the audience when he confesses, "I feel pretty much the same way."

Finally, the executive expresses his own optimism, a basis for providing hope to others. Not with false rah-rah "I know we can do it!" cheerleading. Instead, he provides concrete information—we have new leadership, a large customer base, and so on. He is expressing his own heartfelt hope, providing a basis for others to also feel hopeful.

This snippet of dialogue between an employee and an executive shows how winning minds, hearts, and spirits are intertwined and are not separate phenomena. Story, feeling, and soul—a leader's artistic materials—are all at hand, the executive has equal facility with all three, and he is able to distinguish when his own mind, emotions, and spirit are called for to connect with and win mind, emotion, and spirit from others. He is practicing the discipline of centering, inviting everything that is present to contribute: both frustration and hope, both ideas and emotion, both his own inner world and the inner worlds of the people in his audience. Together, they are playing, as M. C. Richards wrote, "dramatically in the tides of inner and outer, self and other, in an instinctive hope towards wholeness."

Vision and Rendering Significance

"When I first came to this company," the executive tells the audience, "I sold life insurance. I believed that I was protecting people and their families from financial loss and possibly financial disaster. So it wasn't just about selling insurance. I still believe that is what we do—we protect people and their families. The change will be that we will be able to do it in more ways."

He recalls helping a widowed elderly woman by expediting payment of her claim. He then invites members of the audience to talk about moments at work when they had the sense that they were doing something larger than selling and serving insurance policies. There are many such stories.

Here the executive elucidates his own personal vision of protecting people and their families and connects it to the new vision of the company. He has also made a call for spiritual commitment—to a larger sense of purpose than simple self-interest. He has rendered spiritual significance to the new direction of the company—*protecting people and their families.* Just as welcoming all ideas creates a sense of intellectual safety, and welcoming all feelings creates a sense of emotional safety, so talking about personal experience of a higher calling creates spiritual safety. When people experience such safety they begin to believe, "I can take the risk to be who I am in this place. My mind, emotions, and spirit are all welcomed and valued here. I can bring all of myself to this purpose." That belief is where commitment begins.

It Starts from the Heart

The semifictional executive described above has unknowingly followed the advice of improvisational violinist and composer Stephen Nachmanovitch, author of the book *Free Play: The Power of Improvisation in Life and the Arts*. Nachmanovitch wrote,

> If you are giving a public talk, it is fine to plan what you might say in order to sharpen your awareness, but when you arrive, throw away your plans and relate, in real time, to the people in the room.[4]

In contrast to the tale above, Chapter 6 told about an executive whose anxiety over speaking to a large group without a script overwhelmed him. His difficulties did not stem from not knowing the story he was supposed to tell. He knew it intimately; he had helped to create it. What he did not know was how to replace a script as his primary reference point for what to do and say. Once a leader is pledged to an atmosphere of improvisation and a dialogue that carries emotional and spiritual substance, no script will suffice.

The tale in Chapter 6 did have a good ending. On the day of the meeting, immediately after his opening gaffe, the executive sought counsel about the difficulty he was having. He discovered that he held deep convictions and far more than superficial knowledge about parts of the overall story that he was supposed to tell. Heeding the advice of others, he decided to focus on those parts of the story, on the parts that he cared about and could speak about in an extemporaneous way. By the end of the daylong meeting he had transformed fluttering eyelids into appreciative applause.

Where emotional commitment and spiritual commitment are at stake, the heart and soul replace the script.

This "relating in real time" that Nachmanovitch describes must happen everywhere in a leader's realm; not just in front of an audience, but also in the day-to-day business of relating to others as a leader. In every discussion and decision. In every public act. Michael Jones described throwing away the plans and relating in real time as, "Moving from trying to perform according to a preset idea to being more present to the moment so that you are available for what is unfolding in the moment."

The essence of such improvisation is creating with whatever materials come to hand. In the intertwined arts of winning mind, emotion, and spirit what comes to hand are the thoughts, feelings, and soul energy of the leader and the other people present. What is created is commitment. The materials are of two kinds—outer and inner. The outer material is provided by the environment and the people in it. At the meeting described earlier, the outer materials included such things as graphs and charts, questions and comments from the audience, and the mood in the room. Improvisation most often involves responding to those outer materials from the inner materials, what we ourselves think and feel, and the hum of the soul. Sometimes it involves only the inner materials, and it shows up as impulses to speak or act. Nachmanovitch says, "What we have to express is already with us, *is* us, so the work . . . is not a matter of making the material come, but of unblocking the obstacles to its natural flow."[5]

Yes, preparation is needed. But so is an act of letting go of what has been prepared. Artists speak of this improvisational ability in prosaic ways. Painter and art teacher Robert Henri wrote, ". . . if you can at least to a degree free yourself, take your head off your heart and give the latter a chance, something may come of it."[6] M. C. Richards stated, "We have to realize that a creative being lives within ourselves, whether we like it or not, and that we must get out of its way, for it will give us no peace until we do."[7] Michael Jones wrote, "When I place the source of life outside myself, it is easy to feel restricted; I feel lifeless and dull. But when I follow what is flowing from within and trust it, I have never been abandoned; the well is always full."[8] Matt Catingub used to teach jazz improvisation but gave it up. He says, "If you look at where jazz came from, if you look at who created it, they didn't learn it out of a textbook. They didn't learn it because you are supposed to play this scale over this chord."

Improvisation is crucial to centering. A leader's improvisational ability demands mastery of the other leadership competencies, any of which might be called upon at any moment. Improvising artists, such as Nachmanovitch and Catingub or Robin Williams or Charlie Parker, can spontaneously produce seemingly magical acts of creation. When a leader has mastered the competencies for winning mind, emotion, and spirit, and is also able to spontaneously call on them, she is also capable of performing such magic.

Development Strategies for Centering

Centering is not a technique but a way of thinking and being. It is no simple discipline to practice or master. It involves, at the very least, developing a centering consciousness and learning to improvise.

Developing Centering Consciousness

The first challenge in developing the centering consciousness that fosters high commitment is to become aware of habitual ways of thinking and then knowing that there is an alternative. Habitual ways of thinking are very comfortable, personal, and interior mental routines which most people do not even notice in themselves. Here are a few of the ways in which leaders habitually think; they are all aspects of centering consciousness.

- Focusing on commonality as well as difference
- Seeking opportunity as well as problems and obstacles
- Focusing on learning
- Concentrating on accepting or changing self
- Sharing rather than withholding both information and feelings
- Focusing on listening and understanding rather than explaining or defending
- Looking to the present and the future as well as understanding the past

• Assuming an optimistic view

Centering consciousness is the antithesis of the consciousness that separates and classifies, reducing experience to its component parts in the search for understanding. That latter mind, for example, will insist on seeing mind, heart, and spirit as separate attributes. It may create an agenda for a meeting such as the one described earlier in this chapter that looks something like this: from eight o'clock until eleven o'clock we will win intellectual commitment, from eleven until two (including a break for lunch) we will win emotional commitment, and then from two until five we will win spiritual commitment. Centering consciousness, on the other hand, seeks to connect things, including things that are usually thought to be different. The meeting agenda created by a centering consciousness would allow for the emergence of mind, heart, and spirit whenever they show up, as did the agenda of the actual meeting that was described.

Leaders often benefit from the assistance of others who can help them catch themselves when they are trapped in habits of mind that need change, especially the habits of leaving out and separating rather than bringing in and integrating. Chapter 12 offers suggestions for how to find such help.

Improvising

When asked, "What do you tell people who want to learn how to improvise?" Matt Catingub says it is one of his favorite questions. His advice to aspiring improvisational musicians is, "Once a week, go to Tower records or Borders and pick up your favorite jazz improvisation artist—Charlie Parker or Dizzy Gillespie or Winton Marsalis—and buy three CDs. And listen and listen, and then emulate, play along and listen to what they are doing. Do that once a week because it is ear training. You start learning from that. And you also get a great CD collection." Eventually, he adds, you will learn to hear the sour notes; your ear will tell you what is right and what is wrong.

But all of the training, all of the listening and the emulating, will never be enough because, says Catingub, "Improvisation needs to start from the heart." If it doesn't, "It will be so contrived that no one is going to want to hear it."

Learn everything there is to know about your story. Learn everything there is to know about your self. Watch and listen to other leaders. Then set aside everything you have learned. Be present and receptive in the moment. Pay attention to the various echoes of mind, emotion, and spirit from other people, from your surroundings, and within yourself. Trust yourself—play it your way. Surrender—abandon all hope for a particular outcome and all fear of failure. Give up any desire to control. Lead.

Summary

Centering, the discipline of bringing in rather than of leaving out, allows a leader to win the highest levels of commitment by employing all of his competencies in an improvisational art form. Doing so requires developing the discipline of engaging from moment to moment with experience, and honing improvisational skills.

• • •

Questions About Yourself to Contemplate or Discuss with Others

Who, in your life experience, was practiced at centering?

To what degree are you practiced at centering?

What is it about centering that rings true for your current leadership role?

How important is centering to your further development as a leader?

Notes

1. M.C. Richards, *Centering: In Pottery, Poetry, and the Person* (Middletown, Conn.: Wesleyan University Press, 1989): xviii.

2. Ibid., xx.
3. Ibid., xx.
4. Stephen Nachmanovitch, *Free Play: Improvisation in Art and Life* (Los Angeles: Tarcher/Putnam, 1990): 20.
5. Ibid., 10.
6. Robert Henri, *The Art Spirit*, (N.Y.: Harper & Row, 1984; 1923): 195.
7. Richards, *Centering*, 27.
8. Michael Jones, *Creating an Imaginative Life* (Berkeley, Calif.: Conari Press, 1995): 25.

Towering Conclusions and Further Strategies

Art is the language of depth.

—PETER KOESTENBAUM

t is in the nature of leaders to seek expansion, and so they continually seek to expand their leadership capabilities. In general, there are three approaches that leaders take in order to become better leaders:

1. They play to whatever gift they have been given, using that which already comes most naturally to them and that also produces success.
2. They bring aspects of themselves to their leadership that they previously thought were inappropriate, or that they never thought to bring.

3. They develop new competencies such as those described in earlier chapters.

Playing to a Gift

Matt Catingub is a clear example of a leader who plays to his gift. His enthusiasm for his music, and for delighting audiences, is well known among his fans. The *Honolulu Star-Bulletin* draws this picture: "On stage, Catingub . . . seems everywhere: conducting, playing saxophone, wood-wind, or piano, singing, and bantering with audiences in a talk story style."[1] But his career as a band leader did not begin that way.

Catingub first led a big band in Los Angeles when he was twenty-one years old, having already been a professional musician for nearly four years. He put the band together with seasoned professionals. He says, "Most symphony orchestras in the world are very regimented." Catingub does not like regimentation.

Then he decided to put together a swing band. Rather than do it in the usual way by picking veteran musicians, he toured California colleges and universities to hear young musicians. Here is how he describes the result: "I ended up putting together a band of probably 50 percent really, really great players, 25 percent OK players, and probably 25 percent not so OK players, but because their attitudes were so great I decided to keep them. And that pretty much sums up what I like to see. I would much rather have the enthusiastic younger player, who is willing to work at it than the established veteran who thinks he is so good that they don't need to do anything except show up and find out what time the break is. That was my concept, and it paid off in spades because of what I got. I got a beyond enthusiastic bunch of guys and gals; all they wanted to do was play and make music."

In this story it appears that Catingub was merely deciding on the composition of his band, but there is something else going on as well. Gary Zukav described what else is going on in this way: "Each decision requires that you choose which parts of yourself you want to cultivate, and which parts you want to release."[2] Catingub made conscious use of the self-knowledge that he does not like regimentation and that his gift resides in his ability to communicate his enthusiasm for the music. He not only decided on the composition of the band, he also made decisions about what part of himself he wanted to appear when he lead his orchestra. He did not want the regimented part he so dislikes, but the enthusiastic part that is his gift. In choosing band members he selected those people he wanted to have around him in order for him to lead well, and to bring his own gift forward. He said, "I try to have a very, very loose atmosphere. I like having musicians remember when they first started playing music. What was it they liked about it? It is because it was fun. To me attitude has got to be 80 percent of it."

Kathy Covert is another leader who is aware of and plays to her gift. Covert, unlike Catingub, does not get to select the people she leads. Still, she possesses knowledge of her gift and the ability to bring it to situations when it is needed. She said, "If I have a gift it is the capacity to hold contradictions and to hold the big picture and to hold what is possible." When an organization is going off track, or when difficult questions seem to have no obvious right answer, it can count on Covert to remind it of its ultimate destination. Covert said that a leader must, "Know what the gift is and continue to give it."

A leader's initial success at winning commitment of any kind is often achieved when her gift meets the needs of a group of people. Catingub's gift meets the needs of his musicians and of his audience. Covert's gift is essential to organizations that need to be reminded of where they are headed. Monsignor Dale Fushek clearly expressed the relationship between a leader's gift and her success. He said that God gave him two gifts: "One was courage, because I really am not afraid to fail. The other is the ability to find the right person to do the right job. Those two things have helped me to succeed."

A natural gift may provide the key that unlocks the door to leadership. The gift normally appeals to one or the other of intellectual, emotional, or spiritual commitment. Kathy Covert's gift appeals to the mind; she prompts people to remember the big picture, the story they have agreed to live out. Matt Catingub's and Mary Ellen Hennen's gifts appeal to the emotions. Catingub wants audiences to enjoy hearing the music, and musicians to enjoy playing the music, and Hennen wants to foster hope, to "Get people moving towards doing things that they never thought they could do." Monsignor Fushek's courage is a pull to the spirit; the courage to take risks inspires others to do the same.

Uncovering the Self

The second way that leaders develop is to bring to their leadership some aspect of themselves with which they are familiar, but one others have not experienced. Here is an example. The CEO of a foreign division for a large American company was one of those executives who are sent in to clean up wretched situations. He had been, throughout his career, very successful at doing this. His way of improving these situations was, in his own words, to "kick butt." One member of his management team described him as "abusive." Many members of his management team were afraid of him.

Then he was passed over for a larger assignment. The corporate CEO, his boss, told him that, although they would have loved to have his skills and knowledge in the new assignment, his style had abraded too many people. The new assignment would have brought him home from his foreign outpost to corporate headquarters, something he very much wanted because his children and grandchildren lived nearby. The implication was that some people at headquarters preferred that he be kept at a distance. The CEO told him that his style, although useful to the company, had become career limiting.

During a session with an executive coach he talked about his relationships with his grandchildren, saying, "I spend my time with them enjoying them and helping them to learn." His coach suggested that he try that approach with those around him at work, enjoying them and helping them to learn. He agreed to try it. He asked the people around him about their hopes and dreams, about their career plans and the problems they were facing in their work. He asked how he might help, and he listened and followed through. Two years later he was awarded the assignment he wanted at the corporate headquarters.

Uncovering a hidden aspect of the self allows a leader to bring an entire set of behaviors to a situation that is congruent with both who he is and also with the requirements of the situation. It means uncovering some existing part of the self, not learning new behavior. Too often we bring misconceptions or unproductive habits to our various life and work roles, including our leadership roles. We behave in stereotypical ways, or ways that do not serve us or those around us. Executives and managers are particularly prone to these mistakes because they and their followers have so many preconceived notions about how they are supposed to be, and because they tend to emulate those who managed them in the past rather than seek their own best way.

Self-Development

Leadership, more often than not, requires leaders to extend beyond their natural gifts and previously hidden aspects of themselves. Marvin Israelow's bid for a seat on the Chappaqua school board necessitated that he learn how to advocate for a particular point of view, and how to mobilize people. Mary Ellen Hennen had to exorcise her desire to be in control. Alice Harris had to learn to never be ashamed to ask for help. Kathy Covert had to learn to appreciate the significance of good processes. She said, "Earlier in my career the process was not as challenging . . . now it is a much more complex environment in which leaders exercise their influence." To illustrate what she has had to learn, she quotes management theorist Margaret Wheatley: "We do not support what we do not help to create." Covert has had to learn to lead human processes that are inclusive. She is also aware of other aspects of her leadership that she needs to develop: "One of the challenges of my leadership style is to be more supportive of people who are learning." And she knows intellect is her gift and that it is not enough. She says, "My head is my strong suit. Emotions—that is where I need the exercise."

If you are reading this book from beginning to end and have finished the chapters that describe the ten competencies for winning intellectual, emotional, and spiritual commitment, you probably know what you need to learn—which competencies you need to develop. Figure 12-1 provides a handy summary of the competencies and of the development strategies for each of them. The lists of development strategies are not intended as comprehensive inventories, but as beginning suggestions.

Knowledge of the specific competencies that a leader needs to develop is a good framework for whatever action she might take next. If training is pursued, the training should address those competencies. If further reading is pursued, it too can be targeted at those competencies.

How to Choose a Mentor or Coach

Two of the most popular and powerful ways of developing leadership are to find a mentor and to hire a coach. Jim Wold provided a way to think about the difference between a mentor and a coach: "Mentoring is, 'Be as good as I am.' Coaching is, 'Be all that you can be, which is going to be a heck of a lot better than I am.'" Both are valuable. A mentor ought to be someone who has been in the same or a similar situation to that of the leader, and who mastered the competencies that leader needs to develop. A coach ought to be someone who can help a leader to develop the specific competencies he wants to develop, whether or not the coach has ever been in a similar situation. A coach also ought to be able to help a leader clarify his gift, identify aspects of the leader that have been kept separate from leadership, and help the leader bring those gifts and aspects forward. A coach also ought to be expert at helping a leader see that to which he is blind, ought to help place leadership efforts in the larger context of a whole and balanced life, and ought to have the skills and the courage to give useful feedback.

Feedback, in particular, is essential to any attempt to improve lead-

SUMMARY OF COMPETENCIES AND DEVELOPMENT STRATEGIES

WINNING INTELLECTUAL COMMITMENT

Insight
- Asking a vital question
- Gathering and pondering information
- Reflecting
- Unearthing a passion
- Trusting intuition

Vision
- Articulating a vision
- Steering a group process
- Allowing a vision to emerge
- Adopting a vision

Storytelling
- Exercising imagination
- Relying on imagery
- Risking being a person
- Becoming conversant with myth
- Using every point of contact
- Beginning in the comfort zone

Mobilizing
- Encouraging the right things
- Setting high expectations
- Letting go
- Encouraging the best in others

WINNING EMOTIONAL COMMITMENT

Self-Awareness
- Finding the barriers
- Tuning in to the body
- Slowing discussion down
- Reviewing experience
- Shunning "I feel that . . ."
- Practicing an art form

Emotional Engagement
- Practicing empathy
- Focusing on similarities
- Speaking the unspeakables
- Hanging out

Fostering Hope
- Celebrating success
- Doing the impossible
- Assuming self-responsibility
- Listening to self-talk
- Hanging out with optimists
- Getting a good night's sleep

WINNING SPIRITUAL COMMITMENT

Rendering Significance
- Following your bliss
- Uncovering a moral objective
- Creating sacred autobiography

Enacting Beliefs
- Articulating beliefs
- Connecting actions with beliefs
- Choosing a process

Centering
- Developing centering consciousness
- Improvising

Figure 12-1. Table of leadership competencies and development strategies.

ership. It is a sad fact: The more authority a leader acquires, the more he needs feedback, and the less feedback is offered. Mentors, coaches, trainers, associates, family members and friends, and even rivals and those who are reluctant to follow—all can be sources of useful feedback. New York City's former mayor, Edward Koch, used to roam the city asking, "How am I doing?" Sometimes he heard about what was going well, and sometimes he heard things that he would rather not have heard. But his proactive stance about seeking feedback, if not his method, is valuable for any leader to emulate. In other words, with regard to feedback, leaders ought not wait for it, they ought to ask for it.

Individual mentors and coaches have their own have biases towards mind, heart, or spirit. Leaders should find someone who can help them develop in whichever area they most need to stretch themselves. Over time, any leader may want many mentors and many coaches, each for a specific need.

When looking for leadership trainers, mentors, or coaches, also look beyond the realm of those who call themselves trainers, mentors, or coaches; be sure to also look for experts in specific areas. For example, if competence at storytelling is needed, hire a storyteller or go to a storytelling workshop. If skill at improvising is needed, go to an improvisational actor's workshop or talk with a jazz musician. If the capacity for insight needs development, go on a retreat and practice meditation. Leaders should not allow their own development to be limited by the limits of their trainers, mentors, or coaches.

Genuineness

Whether leaders choose to play to their gifts, or to extend themselves in an act of self-development, or to bring forward some part of themselves they have previously kept out of sight, the new self they bring forward must be genuine. Most people can spot phoniness and will not offer commitment to anyone who appears phony.

Genuineness is not problematic when a leader is playing to her gifts.

Gifts come naturally and spontaneously, and are obviously part of who the leader is. Genuineness is problematic, however, when a leader is developing a new competency to add to her leadership repertoire, or is bringing an aspect of the self forward that has previously been hidden. New behavior is often accompanied by clumsiness. Also, leaders get into routines with the people around them, and changes in a leader's behavior, no matter how well-intentioned, sometimes cause alarm in others. For example, when the executive whose story is told above began to bring his "grandfatherly" self to work, his own assistant worried that he was getting ready to fire her. She was worried because, she said, "He has been unusually nice to me lately."

The best thing leaders can do when they are developing a new competency, or are adding new behavior to their leadership repertoires, or are bringing an aspect of the self forward that has been hidden, is to own up to it. Leaders are human beings, and followers appreciate being let in on this fact when it means the leader is trying to become better at what he does.

Practicing an Art Form

Some quotes stick in the mind after their source is lost and seems unrecoverable. For this author one such quote is, "Never trust a leader who is not also an artist." Or something very close to that. The quote can be interpreted in two ways. The first interpretation is that only those leaders who also practice an art form other than leadership can be trusted. This interpretation rings true. Matt Catingub is a musician and a trusted leader. Bill Strickland is a potter and a trusted leader. Beverly O'Neill directed a choir and is a trusted leader. Pat Croce and Zalman Schachter-Shalomi are trusted leaders who have authored or coauthored books. Each of them has learned something about leadership by practicing an art. The second interpretation is that only leaders who recognize leadership itself is an art form can be trusted. This also rings true. Leaders who are able to win high commitment do appreciate the artistry that leadership entails.

Practicing an art form of any kind develops intuition and insight, and it tests the capacity for vision. A body of work created by a single artist represents that artist's personal story, and, in so far as any work of art is shared with others, it can mobilize them intellectually, emotionally, and spiritually. The practice of any art form will enlarge self-awareness, and will challenge the artist to engage emotionally with his subject, as well as with an audience. Art can render meaning that is deeply spiritual, and can confront an artist and an audience, forcing them to clarify their beliefs. Finally, as M. C. Richards has pointed out, practicing an art form provides a powerful metaphor—centering—that relates not only to leadership, but to the whole of life itself.

Leaders ought to hang out with potters, actors, musicians; with those who create. They need not ask artists about their works, but rather about their process. A leader's process is also intended to create. Yes, a leader's media is different: story, feeling, and soul. Yes, the competencies are also different: those for winning intellectual, emotional, and spiritual commitment. But artists can help leaders learn about the process of creating.

Better yet—leaders ought to practice an art form, a form other than leadership. They can transfer the wealth of learning from whatever art form they choose to their own personal and very unique leadership art.

Four Towering Conclusions

All of the experience, thinking, testing and probing, interviewing, research, discussion, and observation that spawned the understanding presented in this book thus far also yielded four conclusions; their importance towers above everything else that has been said. Each has been discussed or alluded to already, and what follows is a summary by way of ending.

The first conclusion is that people commit to other people, so anyone who wishes to lead, to win the commitment of others in order to create change, must become the kind of person who attracts commitment. This is the lesson, reported in Chapter 4, that Monsignor Dale Fushek learned from Mother Teresa. It is more than a matter of learning competencies. It is a matter of living a life. As Jim Ellis said, "How wonderful would it be if you were known through your life as 'Honest Abe'? How much could you do? Wouldn't that be amazing, to have that reputation?"

The second towering conclusion is that a compelling insight about the needs or aspirations of a group of people is far more important to winning commitment than is a vision. Visions that truly compel are founded on such insights and are faithful to them. The third towering conclusion is that, for the job of leadership, reflection is not time away from the job but an integral part of the job. Bill Strickland said it best: "You have to reflect on why you are doing what you are doing . . . or you are lost."

And the final towering conclusion is that, in order for a leader to win exceptional commitment, equal concentration on mind, heart, and spirit is not optional; it is essential.

Notes

1. Tim Ryan, "10 Who Made a Difference: Matt Catingub," *Honolulu Star-Bulletin* (December 30, 2002).
2. Gary Zukav, *The Seat of the Soul* (N.Y.: Fireside, 1990): 138.

Resources

Interviews

Twenty people were interviewed for *The Art of Winning Commitment*. They are all recognized leaders or people who, by virtue of a particular expertise, have something important to say to leaders. Each of them is thoughtful and articulate about leadership. The interviews were conducted by the author from January through June, 2003.

Odds Bodkin—storyteller and author.

Matt Catingub—conductor of the Honolulu Symphony Pops Orchestra.

Wesley Clark—retired U.S. Army General, former Commander-in-Chief of the U.S. European Command, and CNN military analyst.

Kathy Covert—founder of the GeoData Alliance.

Pat Croce—former President of the Philadelphia 76ers and best-selling author.

Jim Ellis—retired U.S. Army General and former Deputy Commander-in-Chief of the U.S. Central Command, currently Executive Director and CEO of The Boggy Creek Gang Camp.

Vincent Francia—Mayor of Cave Creek, Arizona.

Monsignor Dale Fushek—founder, President, and CEO of Life Teen, Inc.

Dawn Gutierrez—Executive Director, New Way Learning Academy.

Alice Harris—founder and Executive Director, Parents of Watts.

Mary Ellen Hennen—Director for Administration, Minnesota State Lottery.

David Hollister—former Mayor of Lansing, Michigan, currently Director of Consumer and Industry Services for the state of Michigan.

Marvin Israelow—former School Board President, Chappaqua School District.

Michael Jones—pianist, author, and consultant.

Wilma Mankiller—former Chief of the Cherokee Nation.

Beverly O'Neill—Mayor of Long Beach, California.

Rabbi Zalman Schachter-Shalomi—Professor Emeritus at Temple University and founder of the Spiritual Eldering Institute.

Bill Strickland—President and CEO of Manchester Craftsmen's Guild and Bidwell Training Center.

Jim Wold—former Superintendent of the New Richmond School District (Wisconsin), now Executive Director of the School of Education at Capella University.

Bonnie Wright—retired from a thirty-two-year career in a variety of leadership roles for the Red Cross, including CEO of Arizona Red Cross.

Print and Web Resources for Leaders

The following list of resources is not offered as a complete bibliography of sources used in *The Art of Winning Commitment*, or as a comprehensive list of resources for leaders. It is a guide to the resources consulted for the book that leaders might find useful in continuing their own development.

Bennis, Warren. *On Becoming a Leader*. Reading, Mass.: Addison-Wesley, 1989.

Bodkin, Odds. Various writing at <www.oddsbodkin.com>.

Chopra, Deepak. Speech to the Mobius Leadership Forum annual conference at the Harvard Business School, April 11–12, 2002. At <www.mobiusforum.org/deepak.htm>.

Gafni, Marc. *Soul Prints: Your Path to Fulfillment*. N.Y.: Pocket Books, 2001.

Gardner, Howard. *Leading Minds: An Anatomy of Leadership*. N.Y.: Basic Books, 1995.

Goleman, Daniel. *Emotional Intelligence*. N.Y.: Bantam Books, 1995.

Goleman, Daniel, Richard Boyatzis, and Annie McKee. *Primal Leadership*. Boston: Harvard Business School Press, 2002.

Henri, Robert. *The Art Spirit*. N.Y.: Harper & Row, 1984 (1923).

Hollister, David. *On Organizing*. At <www.educ.msu.edu/epfp/dh/main.htm>.

Jones, Michael. *Creating an Imaginative Life.* Berkeley, Calif.: Conari Press, 1995.

Keen, Sam. *Hymns to an Unknown God: Awakening the Spirit in Everyday Life.* N.Y.: Bantam Books, 1994.

Nachmanovitch, Stephen. *Free Play: Improvisation in Art and Life.* Los Angeles: Tarcher/Putnam, 1990.

Pearce, Joseph Chilton. *Evolution's End: Claiming the Potential of Our Intelligence.* San Francisco: HarperSanFrancisco, 1992.

Richards, M.C. *Centering: In Pottery, Poetry, and the Person.* Middletown, Conn.: Wesleyan University Press, 1989.

Richards, Dick. *Worthy Visions Pass One Simple Test.* Louisville, Ky.: Brown Herron Publishing, 2002. At <amazon.com/brownherron>.

Schachter-Shalomi, Zalman, and Ronald S. Miller. *From Age-ing to Sage-ing: A Profound New Vision of Growing Older.* N.Y.: Warner Books, 1995.

Simmons, Annette. *The Story Factor: Secrets of Influence from the Art of Storytelling.* Cambridge, Mass.: Perseus Publishing, 2001.

Sternberg, Robert J. *Successful Intelligence: How Practical and Creative Intelligence Determine Success in Life.* N.Y.: Simon & Schuster, 1996.

Unabridged Communications, "Who Leads? A Report on the Usage of Lead, Leader, and Leadership in Selected Newsprint Media in 1996," a report for Callahan, Smith & Gunter, Inc, at <www.members.aol/breakthruz/leadership.html>.

Index

About the Author

Dick Richards draws upon his rich coaching, consulting, and speaking experience, his considerable skill at getting to the heart of the matter, and his faith in the human spirit to help leaders win exceptional commitment to their insights and visions. He has worked with over fifty organizations of all sizes, in business; social service; health care; and education, in more than a dozen countries, to develop leadership, teamwork, and customer service and to implement strategy. He has led or participated in change initiatives within organizations such as ExxonMobil, Prudential Financial, Bank of America, Hewlett-Packard, Procter & Gamble, and the University of Cincinnati.

Richards has been on the leading edge of efforts to bring feeling and spirit to workplaces since publication of his first book, *Artful Work*, which won a Benjamin Franklin Award as Best Business Book. He was chosen as one of 150 world-renowned business thought leaders and practitioners commissioned to provide essays for the landmark reference book on business and management, *Business: The Ultimate Resource.* He is a frequent contributor to professional publications and Internet publishing, writing about leadership, customer service, change, and life-work.

Three of Richards' gifts, remarked upon by clients of his coaching and change consulting practice, are his abilities to "talk hard about the soft stuff," to create "an unusually effective combination of heart and mind, coupled with business sophistication and a results focus," and to offer a wise, experienced, and empathetic ear as "one of the world's best listeners."

Richards and his wife, Melanie, live in Phoenix, Arizona.

Visit Dick Richards' Web site at
www.theclearspace.com
Send e-mail to
winningcommitment@theclearspace.com